LOVE
& LOCKUP

We Got Work to Do

To: Marcella
Thank you for always
supporting me. I pray that
everyone story be a blessing to you.

Shan White

LIFE
LOVE
& LOCKUP
We Got Work to Do

Compiled by

MICHELLE S. LOVETT

Atlanta, GA

DEDICATION

I dedicate this book to my parents Bennie & Gloria (RIP) Lovett, Donna and Tommy Lovett (both deceased) family, friends, those that are battling illnesses and addictions, lupus warriors, domestic violence survivors, individuals that are currently incarcerated or have been. I salute all fighters that took a loss, regrouped, fought again and never gave up.

ACKNOWLEDGEMENTS

I would like to thank the creator (GOD), who is the head of my life. Thank you for turning my life around and saving my soul. I acknowledge my father, Bennie Lovett, who has truly weathered my storms. Dad, thanks for your continuous love, loyalty, guidance and support. C. Nathaniel Brown, thank you for your daily coaching, mentorship and instructions. Bo-Talley Williams, thank you for blessing Volume 1. Let us continue the fight and spread awareness concerning lupus. Russell Tyson, thank you for sharing your talents, love and faith. I extend my appreciation and thanks to my team for believing in this project. The First Ladies of Life, Love and Lockup (10 DIAMONDS), thank you for collaborating and sharing your stories, reliving situations, praying, uncovering hurt and escaping custody. Thanks everyone for working long nights/early mornings; meeting deadlines; going over and beyond; your dedication; motivation; empowerment; advice; encouragement; expertise; and overall making this possible.

CONTENTS

FOREWORD

Self-love is the truest gift that anyone soul could give themselves. Many people have never heard of the word self-love nor understand the meaning of it, until they have become physically, spiritually, emotionally and mentally defeated. Few of us are very lucky to grow up in a household of real-life WOMEN superheroes, who showed impeccable strength and self-love. It may take some time for some to be OK with committing to themselves and loving themselves first. We must realize as wives and as mothers that unless we take care of ourselves, WE cannot take care of anyone else. I am blessed to be born into strength whose names are Marie Talley Davis (mother) and Carrie Talley Wellington (grandmother) and I pray that all women find and understand their strength and know how powerful it could be when your life depends on it. The vitality of super WOMEN is very important for the next generations. It is important that we lead this world into a good path of life to be present in all living things.

As a child, I did not grow up with a silver spoon in my mouth. My mother and grandmother were single moms raising several children by themselves. Even through all of life's trials and tribulations, I always witnessed humbleness, love, protection, and strength from my mom and grandmother. They always seemed to keep it together and classy no matter how bad it got. I never saw them complain nor cry. They were both the main providers of their households. My grandmother and my mom taught me that even in my darkest times never let anyone see you sweat. They taught me that strength does not only come from being able to LIFT heavy things, but strength comes from the ability to CARRY the heaviest things you deal with in life on your shoulders, on your heart and on your mind. You must carry them in a way that you still sustain who you are and still come out on top. I appreciate the strength and all that I inherited from them. I don't take for granted any part of them, that is now me. Rest in heaven Granny, aka CARRIE TALLEY WELLINGTON.

Shellie "Bo" Talley-Williams
CEO of Blaq Pearl Entertainment
Founder of Balling for Lupus Luvs Foundation
Founder of Teach Her More LLC

INTRODUCTION
MICHELLE S. LOVETT

I was placed into custody and sentenced to the death penalty at birth. As a premature baby weighing only three pounds, my lungs weren't working properly, and I needed a new heart. I came into the world with a long list of medical issues and a well-defined battle ahead of me. But since birth, I was also determined to fight, win and be free.

But struggles followed me all my life. Since 2009, I experienced back-to-back deaths of my mother (2009) and brother (2010), coupled with having a life-changing procedure performed. In 2011, I was diagnosed with fibromyalgia. In late 2012, after doctors ran several tests and I sought multiple opinions, I was diagnosed with lupus.

As if battling lupus and going through Lupron treatments weren't enough, I had to adjust to my father remarrying, dealing with a heavy addiction to pharmaceutical drugs, and an array of other issues. I literally gave up on LIFE, shut LOVE out and became LOCKED UP!

I re-evaluated life and what I really wanted. I walked away from the corporate world and became a business owner in 2011. I've been fighting to live since birth. My parents were told to expect the worst (death). Making it through the night would be a miracle, doctors said. Well, 43 years later, I'm still breathing on my own and the hole in my heart is closed. I truly believe my survival was GOD's divine order. Everything that could have killed or destroyed me, rebuilt me.

I have had an anointing and covering over my life since entering my mother's womb. We are all placed on this earth for a purpose. Forever being a student and realizing we will always have work to do, will assist in creating life stories based on experiences. Tests offer testimonies. Sometimes observation leads to passing judgment, however, in most cases, you receive FALSE READS! I CAN ONLY TELL YOU MY STORY!

Life circumstances and different situations often had me questioning the word LOVE. I couldn't comprehend how I allowed certain people in my space or how I endured the pain many brought to me, (family and so call friends). I wanted to know:

- Why different people were connected to me?
- Why would GOD allow me to become motherless at the age 32?
- How could I divorce my so-called best friend only to endure unhealthy, violent, abusive, controlling, manipulative relationships?
- Why was my life so similar to King David's in the bible?

When my mother, brother and sister died, things became very complex. I didn't understand GOD, LIFE OR LOVE! However, my actions and behaviors cost my freedom. I was taken into custody and sentenced to maximum confinement. Everything I stood for, I fell for. The different shifts that took place in my life mentally, physically, and spiritually, all led me to becoming LOCKED UP! Everything became too much. I went to a dark place. I couldn't see any light. I fell into a deep depression, which caused me to have low self-esteem, lose who I was, and more importantly whose I was (God's). Many times, I even questioned why was I still living?

I started dating, fell in love and three months later, he got incarcerated. However, we had an interesting eight-year, complicated relationship. Today, I don't have to front about anything because my life is an open book. Yes, I look different because I feel different! I realize you can't say you're a champion but look defeated. Now, I can love again because I love me. My selection process when choosing a mate has changed. I finally know my worth! Requirements to sit at my table has changed! Anyone can be a fighter but not everyone can be a champion!

I surrendered all, started my healing process and received deliverance.

Life, Love & Lockup a series designed for women and men who overcame adversity, struggles, addictions, illnesses, and other challenges to become successful. Volume 1, "We Got Work to Do" showcases 10 women and their stories of life, love and being incarcerated − physically, mentally, spiritually or emotionally. Their experiences and resiliency along their journey to freedom is sure to help others heal from their hurts and motivate and encourage people in search of their destiny and freedom. In Volume 2, I'll share details about my eight-year relationship and his incarceration; what triggered the restoration of my relationship with my father; my journey and process of becoming drugfree; the sudden loss of my sister; and what happened in my life throughout that storm.

My prayer is after you read this book and subsequent volumes, you will understand the fight. We all will fall down a time or two. However, our bounce back game must be powerful as you will see through the stories of these 10 powerful women with 10 real-life testimonies in Life, Love & Lockup Volume 1 – We Got Work to Do.

CHAPTER 1

LAMECIA KING
MY SMILE CAME AT A COST

As the baby and only girl of three siblings to parents who are still together, I felt like I was entitled to the world. My daddy gave me any and everything I wanted, thought I wanted and could even dream I wanted. He said, "Baby, you don't have to get with a man to get nice things, or because of the car he drives or the jewelry he wears." As a young girl, my daddy showered me with nice jewelry, cars and my own money. He taught me I can have whatever I wanted on my own, as long as I worked for it. I didn't have to depend on or rely on a man to do it for me.

My parents taught me at the age of 3 about being an entrepreneur... from running the family convenience store to selling and sewing cloths with my mother to riding in dump trucks and bobcats while tearing down buildings with my daddy's company, AK Grading and Hauling Inc. My daddy was my knight in shining armor. Like I said, he gave me everything. My parents tried to prepare me for adulthood and protect me from hurt and harm.

But life could not protect me from what was happening. Because I was sheltered. I didn't have street sense nor was I used to the mental games that guys played. I found myself in one relationship after another, constantly wondering what was wrong with me. I questioned why my relationships weren't working. I felt like I didn't have to be in a situation I wasn't happy being in. I didn't want to settle just to say I'm in a relationship or a marriage. For what? To look good to the public and to be miserable for the rest of my life? I was spoiled and was used to getting things my way and if it wasn't my way, I left.

I started comparing myself to others and found myself in a deep depression after two failed marriages and two kids. I found myself being very angry and having outbursts of crying spells.

Wait! Hold the hell up! This was not the life I had envisioned for myself. Still, I kept smiling, kept working and being positive. All hell was breaking loose on all ends. Lost jobs. Lost house. Lost cars. And I was a single mother. My life was in a downward spiral. But I always held on to that tiny hope that God was going to make it alright. I read bible quotes, sung church songs, shouted and cried in church. But when I went home, I faced the same hell. I started to search for inner peace and came across some information on the law of attraction and manifestation. Now this was all new to me. I started practicing and using it daily and wow, it was working. I was happy my kids were happy. I had my house, the dog, the picketed fence, my own business, and my own hair growth product line. I started to manifest things of my dreams. I was an entrepreneur once again, living the life. I didn't need anything. Everything was GREAT!

I was flourishing so I guess life figured it would take me on a ride. I found myself conversing with this guy, who was not my type or anyone I would normally give the time of day. I'm 5'2" and was attracted to the sexy, tall, athletic, muscular, distinguished type of guys. You know the type I mean, the ones in the grocery store who see you on your tiptoes trying to reach for the bread on the top shelf and he appears behind you wearing his workout gear, smelling so divine and fresh. As he leans over behind you, with a deep voice, he whispers in your ear, "Don't worry love, I got that for you." YES, THAT KIND!

Trying not to judge a book by its cover, I gave him a chance and we started dating. Like any relationship when it starts, it was great. I was in love. But there was a thin line between love and hate. Conversation was good. We laughed and had things in common. He offered and promised so many things and I fell for the game. I was in bliss with the ideas we talked about and the plans we made for me to work in Los Angeles as a hair stylist and the deals that he was going to get me. I got sucked in deeper and deeper. Then as time went on, I noticed that we were no longer making plans for LA, nor was he making the phone calls for the deals that he promised me.

I had given up my place, broke my lease, moved in with him and let my children live with their fathers so I would have the flexibility to travel back and forth to LA. Allowing my kids to live with their fathers was the hardest thing in the world for me to do. I got ridiculed and backlash from my family. I felt like a horrible mother. I was only trying to make sacrifices now so my kids would have a better life later. But my family could not understand why I made those decisions. I didn't make my children by myself so why should I have to continue to take care of them by myself and put my career on hold when they have two healthy, willing fathers that were ready and happy to have them while I traveled.

Mind you, I never asked for any of the things this man promised me. He came in the relationship offering. By this time, my credit score had dropped, resulting from the lease he asked me to break and bills that were left unpaid that he promised to pay. He never did. I didn't know he had previously stalked my Facebook page and found out what I was involved in and what I liked. I was too blind to see what was really going on. I started asking about LA and the phone calls to all the so-called connections he had. He yelled. "Stop asking me about the f'ing deals and phone calls. You ain't ready! Don't ask no more!" he

20

said.

He stopped wanting me to go and be involved in red carpet events. He didn't want me to hang with my friends. All of a sudden, he didn't want me to go on set to film or style. He would discredit everything I did.

We spoke about me being a hairstylist for and going to the Golden Globe Awards, Oscars, Grammy Awards, Academy Awards, and SAG Awards. Then his statements turned into: "You have such a small mindset to even think about or want to go to something like that!"

Now whatever I was doing was a problem. When I left the house, I was consistently accused of cheating EVERYDAY. This man was the most insecure human I had ever run across. While trying to film or style on set, I would get multiple phone calls asking when I was coming home. He'd say, "I'm hungry. I want food. This is some bull. You been gone all day? Who you f'ing on set?" Then came the bashing. "You don't do anything for me. You are worthless to me and you add no value to me." Remember, I had given up my place; I didn't want to go back to my parent's house or even let them know what was happening to me.

So, I felt like I was stuck. He controlled the finances and momentarily me. I had lost who I was and what I stood for. I was ultimately and completely embarrassed, ashamed and hurt. Then, this manipulative being had the nerve to say, "You always playing the victim." Manipulators and abusers will always find ways to make you feel it's your fault or you are the one in the wrong.

This man took everything from me... the car, my happiness,

my self-worth, and my peace. How could Lamecia King, Ms. Life Coach herself, get sucked into this bottomless pit of a hell hole with a dude like this who wasn't even worth looking at, let alone talking about being with. The worst was when he started to drink. He didn't love himself or cared about his wellbeing or health. He definitely didn't give a damn about me. He would relive bad experiences during his childhood and take it out on me in a drunken stupor. He would say how unhappy he was and wanted to give up on life. The mental abuse would escalate and go on for hours with name calling, the bashing, and the cursing. I would always leave before it got physical because I knew it was heading that way. He had a history of domestic violence.

Obviously, he didn't want to live so he could care less about my life. I found myself looking in the mirror crying because I didn't even recognize myself anymore. I was in a dark place. When I was around him, I would mentally detach myself from reality and go on a journey deep in my head. I didn't know who this person was, but she was bitter, angry and in a revengeful, spiteful state of rage. She would blank out and not remember what she did. I didn't know what this person was capable of doing. Hell, I didn't even care. After all, I was in an altered state of mind and had no control of her.

The energy this man brought out was evil and unforgiving, a side never seen before and I was scared of her because I didn't know what she would or wouldn't do. She had no fear.

I found myself in this altered state more often than not. I wanted out so bad that I wanted this man DEAD! The anger and vindictiveness would come out of me because I felt betrayed, misled, lied to, manipulated, abused, deceived, embarrassed, and ashamed that I had allowed this poor excuse of a so-called human to do this. There would be days where my focus would be waiting on his death so I could get out this relationship. Yes, I was the same positive thinking, smiling person still trying to give positive affirmations to others but I was struggling with my own stronghold.

I finally started confiding in my best friend about this situation. Now, my best friend is from the streets and has plenty of street smarts and is a businessman. He has been my ride or die since 10th grade. We've seen and been through hell and back together. He has always been there to tell me whether I'm right or wrong, to encourage me, give constructive criticism or lend a shoulder to cry on.

He said, "Mecie, he's trying to treat you like he a pimp and you the hoe. I got friends that are REAL pimps and this is what they do. I love you too much to see this n---a do this to you. So, I'm about to give you a game plan to get out." He was mad that I didn't share this with him earlier. It wasn't pride that wouldn't allow me to share; it was shame and embarrassment. So, I took his advice and followed his instructions while I was in that energy-sucking hell hole. I stacked about $6,000 to $7,000 in a few months, borrowed a friend's car, stayed a few nights in my salon, worked night and day, hired a credit repair company, found a nice spot, signed a new lease and counted down until my place was ready to move in. The whole time, I was still under his roof. I couldn't worry about the abuse or my feelings at the time because my mission was bigger.

So, when he decided to tell me to get out AGAIN... O BABY, I was ready and so was my place... just in time. He wasn't expecting me to be on my ish. He thought he still had me mentally and financially incarcerated and it was going to be one of those typical nights I leave and go to my salon just for some peace and quiet. The next few days my oldest brother moved me into my new place. Bad credit, didn't own a car, had to buy new furniture and everything but I was ok with that because I was happy and I had peace and a peace of mind, which is priceless.

See, when the devil thinks he got you right where he wants you, God steps in and has a ram in the bush waiting for you. I had to remember that I am the daughter of the Most High. My last name is not KING by accident. Not only did I feel like I was locked up physically, I was shackled mentally. I had to break the cuffs of my own inner thoughts and forgive myself. Often, we cause more mental abuse on ourselves by not forgiving ourselves for the decisions we made. I have learned that I cannot change the past, but I can make better decisions right now to avoid repeating the same mistakes. No one comes into our lives by accident. I thank God for every person that has come into my life, who is in and who has left. Without them, I would not be the strong woman I am today. I appreciate the situations I went through. It was all necessary for this birthing process. When we change how we look at things, the things we look at change. You cannot give birth without pain. You have to get dirty, be broken, beaten, emptied and bruised in order to appreciate and reap the rewards of your labor. Your sacrifices, patience, tears, pain and prayers are not in vain. Don't give up and don't give in. You are more powerful than any of the strongholds. Remember, the day you plant the seeds will not be the day you eat the fruit. What has helped me to be able to forgive myself and the individuals who have wronged me, is knowing that no matter what they have done or continue to do, it's not going to stop or change God's blessings and promises for me.

I practice the law of attraction daily. Be mindful that practicing the law of attraction does not stop things from happening to us. But by us changing our mindset and changing how we react to what has happened could change the outcome of the situation. Meditation, crystals, gems, sage, essential oils, meditation music and herbal remedies are some properties that help my energy stay in harmony and at peace even when outside forces and energies are present. By separating myself from negative energy and having gratitude for what I have has made manifesting my desires easy. My company, Zhazar LLC, has taken off in ways only imaginable. Zhazar hair growth line and men's beard line called Full Beardz are being sold worldwide. This is only the beginning and the surface has not even been scratched yet. My smile is big because its mine and I paid the price for it.

Every day, we are constantly evolving and changing so I pray this prayer every day: "Lord, guide me. Allow me to be a blessing to someone today. Have me to do what you want me to do. Add the people to my life that you want me to have and please remove those from my life that do not belong. Amen."

This has changed my life. I believe it will change yours also.

Lamecia King is a celebrity hairstylist and owner of Zhazar Hair Studio in Atlanta. In addition to being an entrepreneur and haircare products developer, she is a certified life coach, cranial prosthesis specialist and actress. The mother of two daughters, Lamecia enjoys volunteering with several community organizations that serve the homeless population and children. She also works with the American

Cancer Society through a program called Look Good Feel Better. As an actress she has appeared in several commercials, television shows and movies. Her motto is: "God has blessed me so I can be a blessing to others!"

CHAPTER 2

CATRESE DAVIS
UNPLUG OBSESSION
TO UNLOCK FREEDOM

In my life, I was driven by the obsession to be loved and my freedom to love me was locked up because of trust issues and not knowing how to love me. Eventually, after countless mistakes, hurting myself, and unintentionally hurting others, my freedom to love me and be me was unlocked.

From the time we are born, we encounter circumstances with someone who will make us feel good or feel bad or make us feel inferior or make us feel inadequate. We become shaped and developed into multiple personality dysfunctions and positive emotional functions that create life situations. Our lives have been based on the image we want to portray to those around us but we hide reality. We all have been ashamed of things we have done, said, and forced to experience. The reason we experience delayed success and delayed happiness is because we deny reality and refuse to communicate our truth. All we have done is defend or validate ourselves to everyone around us. Open your eyes. Whenever your eyes are open, you can see how much light there is and how dark there is, in what direction to walk to avoid bumping into things and how everything appears to be operating before you. When your eyes are closed, you can see nothing and if you move with your eyes closed, you are immediately at risk of damaging yourself. As long as we live on earth, we will always have some type of relationship with another human being and it will affect our life in a positive and/or negative way, intentionally and unintentionally.

As a child, I felt abandoned, rejected, unwanted and like someone was always taking from me something or someone that I loved. I could not understand why I did not have a mother or father. At five years old, my mother was murdered, and that man took away part of my heart and being. My father chose not to be in my life. My grandparents took my brother and me to raise us so that we would not be in the foster care system. However, my grandparents were an old age; my grandfather died during my 7th grade year and my grandmother died after I graduated from high school. I had no idea what I was about to encounter in life. I was determined to live a life of love and I dived in relationship after relationship and marriage after marriage. After all the relationships and marriages throughout my life that failed because of the slightest betrayal, I felt like a failure and left. If given another chance to be in love, I was determined that my love for stability and romance would keep me from being so quick to run after betrayal.

Well, I was given another chance but I was not ready. It was my youngest daughter's birthday and I was on my way to pick up my daughters and their friends. As I was driving and feeling lonely after being single for a year, I began to pray. Tears rolled down my face. I cried out to God: "Please remove this loneliness because I need to be loved but if it's not meant for me to be with anyone then I will accept that. But if you give me someone, I want a tall, good looking man who will love me. He does not have to go to church but as long as he knows and loves you, God, then I'm fine with that. I don't want a weak man so make him strong and tough and fun. If you do that, I will not leave so quickly if something goes wrong. In Jesus's name. Amen."

We must be careful what we pray for. We most definitely need to be healed from past baggage and prepared for what we ask God to entrust us with in our lives. Well, I had no idea my prayer would be answered the same day. I picked up the girls and we drove around on Candler Road to pass out flyers inviting people to church. I prayed with a few people as I was teaching the girls evangelism.

We were on our way to the nail salon so I could get their nails done. I stopped on Flat Shoals Road to get gas. My daughter said I needed to wash my car and that there was a $3 car wash across the street. So, after I pumped the gas, I drove to the car wash and realized the $3 car wash sign was a bold-face lie. However, I needed my fully loaded, pearl colored car with the sunroof and shining rims detailed so I drove up to look at the prices. There was a handsome man looking at us as he was getting his burnt orange old school car detailed. After my car was finished, I was walking across the parking lot and I looked his way. He lifted his hands in the air as to gesture, "What's up? Can I come talk to you?" I gestured back by throwing my hands up and motioned for him that it was fine for him to come to me. The girls said he was cute so go for it. I shook my head at them as I was nervous. He walked over and spoke to all of us and introduced himself and I did the same. He explained his current status (that I will not detailed here). I was impressed with his honesty. We laughed as he looked at our reflection in the window and said, "We look good together." He said I looked like an angel walking across the parking lot and everything around him stopped. I smiled and felt a flutter in my belly. I gave him a flyer and invited him to church and he was amazed as he stated he was looking for a church to attend. He gave me his number and we left the carwash.

The girls were telling me to make sure I called him but I was somewhat skeptical. Later that day, I called so he could have my number. He later informed me that he gave me his number so he could see if I was interested instead of him getting my number, calling and running the risk of being rejected if I weren't interested. We talked for hours as we laughed and shared so many things. He took me out every day for months and we were like Bonnie and Clyde. We were attracted to each other mentally, physically, and spiritually. We fell in love and could not get enough of each other as we took millions of pictures, made love in untraditional places being spontaneous, and going to church together to worship God. But things began to spiral out of control when my past baggage began to interfere.

My stepson from a prior marriage was living with me as his dad had moved in with another woman before we divorced. It became chaotic because my ex had begun to rebuild his relationship with the kids and they began to act differently towards my new man. My new man was watching how the chaos was unfolding and tried to warn me but I refused to listen because I wanted to protect my children's hearts after they had experienced depression and devastation from the divorce. I wanted them to be healed even if it meant rebuilding their relationship with my ex. However, it caused major issues between me and my new man, who had swept me off my feet and made me feel alive again after being in a deep depression that almost killed me. I noticed his behavior changed, even though he moved in the home with me and he tried to tell the kids things to help them. But because he was so blunt, they began to rebel even more. They hated his approach and felt he was trying to be their father and they were not having it. I was caught in the middle. I didn't want to lose my man or my children.

Nevertheless, the cheating had begun and I felt it deep down in my spirit. The signs were all there as I noticed him turning over his phone when he had specific incoming calls, late night calls became frequent, and he stayed out late without me. I would wake up in the middle of the night watching him text then try to hurry up and put the phone down. I addressed him about what I discovered and he denied any wrongdoing. One day, he called me to send him his resume from his computer. I had no idea what I was about to see would blow my mind. He had forgot to close his secret file and I saw a lot of his past with explicit pictures. I was blown away. It made me look through other files and that's when I saw the selfie picture of him with his mouth to another woman's ear and neck at a bar. I know it was while we were together because the hat he wore was purchased when he and I went to the mall. I felt all types of emotions and I was hurt. I confronted him and he tried to lie and give me all types of excuses. We argued and I decided to let it go and make up. It was the best sex ever.

We had moved on from that incident and one day we were watching the TV show *Cheaters* because he loved it and told me to check it out. At the end of the episode, they talked about trackers and he turned to me and laughed as he said, "Do not ever put me on *Cheaters*." I took that and began to analyze it. I researched trackers and spy devices. Guess what happened next? I made up in my mind that I was going to see if he had been lying to me. I did not truly realize I was about to become obsessed with trying to hold on to him by invading his privacy, as I tried to control him from cheating. I was damaged in the process and in turn damaged him, too. We both had our freedom locked up.

One night, I had candles everywhere and rose petals from the bedroom door to the garden tub and from there to the bedroom. The music filled the room creating an ambience of sensual breathtaking love. We had passionate sex. I waited until he fell asleep and was snoring then unlocked his phone and downloaded the WebWatcher app, which at the time would show his location, text messages, recorded phone conversations, and Facebook messages. I had access to all of him and was determined to find out what he was doing. No need to give all the details, but I caught him at multiple women's houses, read text messages that hurt my heart, and saw pictures that women sent him of their body parts. I was hurt and relieved at the same time because I finally knew the truth. But it damaged me even more. I became obsessed with thinking I could get him to stop if I kept showing up and calling these women to let them know who I was. Some of the women had no heart and others were very remorseful.

He became so angry with me that domestic violence soon followed. One day, I tried to figure out which apartment he was in and tried to call the cousin he said he was with. The location appeared different from what he told me. When he came out, the tug of war began. Other incidents included him snatching my wig off and throwing it out the window while we argued; pressing his hand over my mouth so hard that it caused my teeth to cut my lips; throwing me on the ground, scraping my knees and arms; and so much more. We began to fight more than ever but we just could not let each other go. We always made up as we tried to figure out how we had spilled over into this place of chaos. We were both locked up and had no idea how to get our freedom from this chaos. We both needed to learn how to love ourselves and not search for validation from others. We had to unplug our obsession to unlock our freedom. We both had an obsession in our lives that we felt were solutions to our life circumstances when it only damaged both of us. It kept us locked up from the freedom to be who we are instead of what everyone wanted us to be. All our lives, we tried to please others when it only created more issues within ourselves. After years of back and forth obsessions then getting married and continuing the cycle, we finally unlocked our freedom. It was not easy for us to end our marriage, but it was time to heal as we both knew it was for the best. We continue in our healing as we talk to each other about our past errors and have forgiven each other. We are embracing who we are now and dealing with those inner issues that almost destroyed us and some of it stemmed from our childhood. We have taken the time to identify those areas and face the truth so that we can be truly free. Are you free?

Some of us were born by way of fornication, adultery, rape, and/or marriage. We were created through humans by love, lust, anger, or mental illness. Therefore, we were treated specifically by the emotions of the parent depending on their psychological mindset of whatever situations they experienced in their life. We all have purpose and how we are treated will affect our lives in a tremendous way. We have judged many and only created more anguish with no rehabilitation. Therefore, we leave the door open for it to happen again! We have the ability to be real about our image in the present and open our eyes to reality of who we really are and make adjustments to bring great communication, understanding love, and success in every aspect of our lives. Unplug your obsession to unlock your freedom.

Catrese Davis is CEO of Nu Level Generation Services Inc, Le'bleu Diamond Cosmetics, Real Boss Connections and LWV Ladies With Vision, a non-profit organization. Before moving to Atlanta, Catrese was born in Newark, NJ, and lived in Williamston, NC. The author holds an Associate's degree in business and a Bachelor's degree in religion. She has worked in human services for over 20 years and in public relations. In her spare time, she is a motivational speaker, co-hosts The Talk Show Divas, implements give-back events in the community, substitute teaches, and acts. She believes if you have a vision, it can become a reality.

CHAPTER 3

BRIDGETTE DENISE
SHE LOOKS JUST LIKE ME

It was a night that I will always remember, the night they violated me. I can still see it vividly. The stench of funk mixed with cologne and alcohol was sickening. I started to scream and try to wiggle myself out of his reach, but he wasn't by himself. It was three of them. They held me down while ripping off my clothes to have their way with me, at the same time bashing my head and pistol-whipping me until I passed out.

Life for me ain't been no crystal stair... It's had tacks in it and splinters and boards torn up and places with no carpet on the floor, bare... (Langston Hughes)

I didn't have what you would call a great childhood. I know you are saying, "Well, neither did I" or most people do not have a great childhood. As far back as I could remember, I have dealt with trauma. I had a tumultuous upbringing, being raised in a two-bedroom apartment where I shared a room with three other siblings along with my mother who raised us by herself. I can remember a time as a kid I thought life was gravy, outside of the whoopings and beatings that we received. But as I look back, I came to look trauma in the face at an early age. It feels as if trauma and I have been friends for a long time.

Grief and pain gripped my soul at a young age. You see, I can vividly remember looking death in the face, only a few steps away from me. I became best friends with trauma and suffering at the time I didn't know what was really in store for me. Nor did I understand what was actually taking place in my life. Growing up in the ghetto of Atlanta, as I knew it, was what I experienced and where I would find myself in life. But God had a different plan.

It had been a great day at work. It was extremely busy. The vibes were good with the crew and even management had jumped in and made things happen. This hot summer day was winding down and I was ready for my shift to be over. The manager came up to me and asked if I could close the store because one of my co-workers had called in (just my luck). I called my brother to see if he could meet me to walk with me since I knew it would be late and dark. At that time, Buford Highway was a bunch of woods with a few stores and apartment complexes here and there. He agreed and told me to call him before we were leaving.

When my shift was over, I called my brother and he said he was on his way and would meet me halfway. I started walking, which wasn't new for me. I noticed three men walking behind me. I felt something in my gut and crossed the street. They followed me. I walked faster wondering when I would see my brother and feel safe. As I tried to cross back to the other side of the street, I felt someone snatch me up. His breath reeked of alcohol. I was fondled. I felt a humiliating feeling coming over me as I tried to scream and was grabbed by my neck and his hand went over my mouth.

"Shut the f--k up, bi--h. You better not scream, or I will blow your f--king head off," he said.

I was dragged into the woods as I was being pistol-whipped. I tried to wiggle myself out of his grip, but it was three of them. They held me down and ripped off my clothes to have their way with me. They beat me until I passed out. When I came to, I was in a strange place. The police were there and I freaked out. A couple coming home from the movie theater

(Cinema 12) saw me in the woods and called the police. They took me to their house and the police was there when I came to. I was questioned, placed in an ambulance and taken to the hospital where I was treated as if I brought this on myself. I was not only violated but humiliated. I was questioned about why I was out so late. They said, "Why didn't you catch a cab?" They said things like, "She's probably one of those fast-tailed girls we see all the time crying victim." I was sitting there wondering, "Where is my brother?" He was asleep at home.

"What's love got to do with it?" was the question that Tina Turner asked and believe it or not I have that same question. I've travelled down the road of love maybe once or twice. Well, actually more than that and that time I really thought I had found someone just for me. But in time love will tell me a different story.

I never would have thought that the things that I've endured would have such a major impact on *every* aspect of my life. You see, it would be later in life when I realized that after the rape, a chain was wrapped around my mind that hindered me from trusting any man... and woman, too. I was bound in my thoughts because of the trauma that I had endured. Statistics say that when people are violated (raped and molested), they often turn to being promiscuous. However, I didn't realize that just because I didn't turn to sleeping with any and everybody, I became promiscuously bound in my thoughts. I developed psychological warfare in my own mind. I became my own enemy. Lacking the presence of a father and not knowing how to handle what I had become, I became increasingly depressed without anyone ever knowing. Suicide was my constant thought and I even tried to take my own life.

As I became what I considered an adult, I pushed everything to the back of my mind, got involved in the church as much as possible, and was still making bad decisions. I found myself in verbally abusive relationships one after another. It never got physical, but the mental abuse would begin to weigh on me as the years past. It appeared that I had it all together, but on the inside, I was a volcano ready to explode with anger, resentment, hurt, anguish, and pain, amongst other emotions. I was still in the choir singing praises unto to God, still on the Usher Board and I had even answered my call to become a minister in the Lord's house. I know you are probably saying that's not right. I did not understand what God was really doing in my life. I thought I knew. I even got married and thought that God was going to bless my union, not knowing that this would be a period of hell opening the doors in my life.

I was a silent victim of marital rape without anyone knowing. At the same time, my then husband was playing the organ and keyboard and conducting the choir and praise team every Sunday. That was just another brick to the house of pain that would later turn into my house of praise.

I met this man named Calvin. He was very well known in the community, a playwright, a surgical technician for a well-known hospital and a business owner. From the looks of it, he had his life together. After all, he was a man of God, studying to become a minister so you know I could relate to him and he could relate to me. He told me that he had been watching me for some time and that he wanted to pursue a relationship with me. We hung out a few times trying to get to know one another; we worshipped together; he prayed for me and I prayed for him; and we even went to Tybee Island for a short vacation (where he mysteriously left his wallet at home). I really thought we could have something together but oh how I was wrong. The tables would soon turn. He never had enough. He was always struggling after we came from Tybee Island. He lost his car, lost his apartment and it seemed as if I had to spring into action to help him. I mean, after all, he was my man, right? I extended my home to him so that he could save money to move into him another place. Then it happened. The wool came off. What was really there was exposed and who he really was was revealed.

My heart was wrapped up in this man only to find out what was really lurking in the darkness. I noticed things early on but because of who he was on paper and in the community, I didn't want to believe the signs. I was at my best friend's house for her birthday celebration and I received a phone call from an unknown number that morning around 8 a.m. I didn't answer it the first few times they called. Whoever it was kept calling so I finally answered it. It was a female's voice on the other end asking to speak with Angelita. I said, "This is she," and the caller replied, "The d--k was good, bi--h!" I said, "Good for you!" and hung up.

She continued to call my phone. I got so annoyed that I answered it only to hear, "Black pants, grey shirt and grey boxers" followed by laughter. I confronted him but he tried to make it seem the woman lying. It was all true and I stayed anyway. Why? Because I was used to the abuse and didn't even realize that I was being abused. He kept cheating. Tonya, the woman who had been calling, kept trying to warn me that Calvin used women for their money and that he was involved in some other activities at the strip club. She even warned me that he was an alcoholic and told me she was pregnant by him. But that wasn't it. Things got even deeper. I went to the doctor's office for my annual checkup only to find out he gave me a STD (Sexually Transmitted Disease) but he also gave me a STD (Spiritually Transmitted Demon). Normally, as women, we would confront the other woman, but I realized she looked just like me... damaged.

After I ended the relationship things got very volatile, to the point where he started stalking me. He would ride by my house and text me as if he was having a conversation with me. The text messages would start by saying how much he missed me and then escalate to him calling me names and saying crazy things to me. It got so bad I was afraid for my life. I bought a gun (9mm Rugger) and filed a restraining order against him. The day I went to Cobb County to file, I received a phone call from an Apostle who didn't know anything about him and these were her words to me: "Who is this person calling you from unknown numbers?" I gave her the woman's name. She proceeded to tell me about my relationship with him and said he made a pact with the devil to destroy me. He was fighting for his life because when you make a pact with the devil and you don't complete your assignment, you are tormented. She told me to go quickly and file the restraining order. "As quickly as he came, he's going to go just that quick," she said.

It took me three months to obtain a restraining order. At this time, he was calling and texting every day, sending me obscene videos and calling me names, visiting my home and making reference to the things outside of my house. It got so bad I called his pastor trying to find some form of relief. The day

I saw him face-to-face in front of the judge, he was very angry. I could see the demons that tormented him in his eyes. I kept every text message and printed them out. He told the judge that I was a liar and I showed the judge my phone with the messages. He kept having outbursts in the courtroom and was almost found in contempt. Needless to say, I was granted the TPO (temporary protective order). Afterwards, I was called an "evil bi--h". I wanted to hate him but I couldn't. I wanted to despise him but I couldn't. The God inside of me wouldn't allow me to be consumed by the very thing I was fighting against. It was then that I realized I needed a spiritual cleansing and that I was facing a generational curse. You see, I had encountered this sex demon and didn't know how to shake it. That wound never healed. The past had somehow resurrected itself and I finally had to face it head on. There was no more running, no more pushing it to the back of my mind. I had to travail. I had to lie prostrate. I prayed. I cried. I denounced every demon that I allowed to become a part of who I was and who I am. I repented for the things I allowed to happen. I forgave myself and I also prayed that God would deliver him and have mercy on him. I prayed that somehow he would find his way back to God. I forgave Calvin but I also realized that I had to forgive myself for the self-inflicted abuse. I had to be honest with myself and realize my true worth. I had been selling myself cheap. I had been giving too many discounts. It was time to be released and heal for real. I started my healing process.

On, May 1, 2018, one of my castmates sent me an inbox message on Facebook Messenger asking me if I was ok. I told her yes and wondered why she would ask me that. She stated, "You don't know, huh?" "Know what?" I replied. "Calvin is dead," she said.

 **Bridgette Denise** is the founder and CEO of Enduring the Cross Ministries and AMcCants Ministries, a licensed counselor, the Dean of Education for the School of the Great Commission, an advocate for Autism, motivational speaker and an actress. Her passion for service and people has brought her to the threshold of changing lives thru the many opportunities afforded in ministry. Her mission in life is to be used by God to infect the world by becoming salt and light (Matthew 5:13-16). She is the mother of one daughter and grandmother of two. She lives in Stone Mountain, GA.

MICHELLE S. LOVETT

CHAPTER 4

LESLIE JAMES
LETTER TO YOU

Dear You,

I was warned countless times, but never heeded the advice. You showed many signs, but I choose to ignore them. You were jealous, your temper uncontrollable. You embarrassed me and made me an emotional wreck every time you'd lose it and it never mattered where we were. Yet, I stayed quiet. Hurt and saddened by your behavior, I would drop my head and just pray.

You could do no wrong, always pointing the finger blaming me for your insecurities. The baggage you brought into this relationship became a part of me.

I remember the night we were sitting on the sofa watching television when I received an email with a picture of you with another woman. I got up to walk away and you walked closely behind me. You noticed the disgusted look on my face. Instead of asking what was wrong or even if I was ok, you said, "What the f--k is your problem." I needed to address it at that moment. I didn't care about the outcome. I handed you the phone and asked you to explain it. You took the phone and said you didn't see a problem with the picture. I didn't want to yell because the kids were in the next room, so I calmly asked, "Why did you lie about the trip to visit your father?" You told me that it was irrelevant and if I continued to speak about it, you'd pack your bags and leave me. I wanted to say, "Get get your sh-t and go!" But I didn't have the strength to do it.

The day you left, the silence during our phone call let me know that something was wrong. I said hello over and over but I couldn't hear anything on the other end. Hoping that you were ok, I just waited for the phone to ring back. A week later, I was excited when I got that call. I didn't hesitate to answer because I wanted to hear all about the trip and get answers. You said the trip was alright. Just alright? You said you had something for me. I asked what it was, and you said a picture of you. It was the same location and pose that was in the photo with the woman I received in my email. You decided to have them cut her out the picture, but they forgot to cut out a part of her hair. I asked why this woman was so close to you and all you could say was that I was f--ked up in the mind and that people were in front of you exiting the boat. I thought well maybe I was tripping, so I left it alone.

Weeks later, I finally got my truth when that same picture came to my email. I guess you thought it would be nice to gift me with a photo of you and this other woman. She was the same woman who you sat in my house, on my sofa, and spoke with while I worked my ass off all day to provide for you. Yeah, I got those emails, too. I allowed you to disrespect me on so many levels. I took verbal and physical abuse for you.

Instead of leaving when I had the chance, I stayed by your side. Although I had been in other relationships, this one was different. I had never experienced so much hurt. You wanted me to believe that no one loved me and all I needed was you. I stayed up at night talking to my family and friends crying my eyes out hoping that they could help me rescue myself from you. When you realize what was happening, you made me cut communication with the people I love. My children were the one thing that brought me peace and kept my sanity in this relationship, but you tried to turn me against them and them against me. With tears in my eyes, I watched my daughter walked away. She told me that I would be a fool if I stayed. I remember the day I introduced you to her and she said to me,

"Mom, something is not right about that man." I wanted to listen, but I felt the need to give you a chance. My son stayed because he was afraid to leave me alone with you. He felt the need to protect me. It was my job to protect them. I let you into their space, where they felt safe. I was vulnerable at the time. I was going through a divorce and I allowed you into my life to fill what I thought was missing. I didn't realize I just invited a stranger into my house.

It took me years to remove the blind fold and get a glimpse of who you really were. And only then did I see just how toxic you were. Even with being a Godly woman, I began to question my strength. I was so focused on trying to build you up that I lost myself. I started to believe that we were all that mattered and I did not need anyone else. There were too many times that I allowed you to manipulate and control me. You made me feel that I was responsible for you, no matter how many times I was told I wasn't. It wasn't long before I realized you weren't just toxic to me but to everybody around you. I tried to fight for you, even with the damage you caused, hoping that you would become the man you claimed to be in the beginning.

Eventually, I had no more expectations. Regardless of the pain, I still refused to acknowledge what was right in front of me. You tried to put fear in me when you raised your fist and raised your voice with the look of satan in your eyes. You caused a high level of stress in my life at the time I was supposed to be healing. When the opportunity presented itself, you took my demons and used them to your advantage. You tried to silence me. I had to think about things before I said them, wondering if I would be beaten or called out my name. I had to walk on eggshells in my own home because your mind was made up...

you wanted to take control of my house with your destructive behavior. You let me know that my opinion didn't matter in a harsh way. You tried to paint a horrible picture of me in the eyes of others. And when I stood up for myself, all hell broke loose. I became crazy and nasty. I became what the other woman wasn't. You compared me to your exes, making me feel that my love wasn't good enough. I lay awake at night doubting myself as a person with tears pouring down the side of my face while I stared at the ceiling and prayed to God to give me strength to let you go. You made so many threats about of leaving because you didn't want me to have a voice. I wasn't afraid of you leaving. I just didn't know how to walk away. You wanted me to be submissive in the midst of the pain.

I had to wear a fashion scarf around my neck to match my outfits because I still wasn't ready to walk away nor did I want to hear what anyone had to say about the deep scratches on my neck and the bruises on my face from you grabbing me, tearing the shirt away from my body. I could feel the impact from being pushed into the TV set that was sitting on a wooden dresser in the hotel room. I was angry. I wanted to fight back. I felt weak and humiliated. Because you can't control your drinking habit, I suffered.

I still stayed and listened to you blame me once again for your insecure ways. You told me you loved me and you would protect me. But you were what I need to be protected from. I thought you would be my cure but you were my disease. You invested absolutely nothing and expected everything, including my apologizing for the way you treated me.
I will never forget the day I brought you to meet my mother. I looked at you as you walked across the living room to greet her.

You wrapped your arms around her and let her know how it was wonderful to meet her. You turned around and walked to the couch. I turned to look at my mother. The look she had on her face as she stared at you sitting there was unfamiliar, as if she didn't trust you. It almost seemed as if she was in a trance. I had never seen that look on her face before. At that moment, I wanted to run and not look back.

I will never forget that look in my mother's eyes. She knew you weren't the one for me but I chose to ignore what was right in front of me. From the moment you walked through my door with your arrogant behavior, lack of empathy for others, and self-centered manipulative and demanding ways, I had a gut instinct that you were wrong for me. I still choose to ignore it. I stopped believing in myself and isolated myself from the people that loved me most. They asked what they could do to help, and I still covered for you. I couldn't trust anymore, feeling that someone would break my heart. Loving you hurt me, and the hardest part was finding my true self again. Because I suffered so much damage, I wondered whether I could love the way I desired or be loved the way I deserved. But I understand that for me to move on, I must forgive you so that I can learn to live again and prepare myself for what the world has for me. So, today, I forgive you and I wish you the best. But I can no longer drown in misery or carry the baggage of your insecurities and inadequacies. I am finding myself again, this time without you.

I had to re-discover my inner strength and take control of my own life. I made the choice to feel love again. I set boundaries and stood up for myself. I was fed up. I was over it. The day you picked up a fireplace iron and threatened me again, and my son had to get involved, I knew I had to had to protect myself and my world, my son. It hurt me to the core to see my son with that much anger and pain from fear that I would be hurt. I decided to let go. I am re-establishing myself, finding parts of me that were pushed aside during that relationship. I am moving things along quickly, establishing new goals and direction. I started to pray more and I know now that in order for me to help others, I needed to find myself. I understand that there are people who don't have support and feel like they're stuck. But at some point, they will thank you, too. Because of my experience with this abuse, I will reach them and help them understand that they are not alone. They, too, will overcome abuse. On behalf of myself and all other victims, I bid farewell to you.

Sincerely,
Me

 **Leslie James** is an American actress, writer, and production designer. Born and raised in Miami, her love for acting came naturally at an early age. Lady M has appeared in numerous stage plays and short films such as Nadia and M.O.M.S. (Mothers of Murdered Sons), which addresses police violence and its impact. She hones her acting skills at Premier Actors Network under the tutelage of Dwayne Boyd. In her spare time, the mother of two and outdoors enthusiast enjoys writing, fine dining, doing makeup, playing tennis and mentoring women and children.

MICHELLE S. LOVETT

CHAPTER 5

TIKITA "TIKI J" FICKLIN
A WOMAN'S CONFESSION

There is something innately inside of us that desires love. But the journey to find true love sometimes starts before you're ready and the road is filled with bumps and bruises, passions and pains, that can take you out or can ultimately lead you to true happiness and walking in divine purpose. But it often comes with a cost.

I was created by God to have a big heart to love and encourage everyone that comes in my presence to be better and reach their full potential. When you are created to bring the best out of others, the enemy will always put people and things in your path to dim your light. I emptied out my love and some took advantage of me and took my kindness for granted. I grew up to be a woman who loved deeply but was still often misused.

At a young age, I gave her heart to Daniel. We met when I was 14 years old and he was 16. I became a mother to my first son at 19, and a wife at 20. I desired to be a wife, a mother, and to have a family of my own. I loved God and wanted to live under the guidance of Christianity. However, my husband was a street guy who gambled, stayed out all times of the night, and was addicted to alcohol. Even after the late nights or if he came home at all, he would throw money at me to supplement for his absence. I continued with the marriage and became pregnant with my second son at 25. It was a difficult pregnancy, due to the stress of loving a man that loved the streets more that he wanted to be a father and a husband. My second son was born prematurely at 29 weeks. The doctors told my husband that an emergency C-section was needed to save my life and our unborn son. I spent many nights crying myself to sleep and stressing about the choices my husband made. Depression and loneliness were as real as my newborn baby fighting for his life in the incubator.

Even though I had an emergency C-section, I still was at the hospital every day providing breast milk for my newborn so he could have a better chance at developing. My baby was so small that he could fit in the palm of my hand. I brought him home in a mini basket because he was too small for a car seat. I loved my baby, spoke life over him, and helped him develop into a strong healthy little human. He grew and I kept pushing on.

After all the disrespect, emptiness, and not being loved properly as a wife, I sought love from another. Now, I'm not saying it was the right thing to do, but at that time, I felt justified. After all the late nights, or days of my husband being away from home, and other women calling his phone, I decided that I would give him a taste of his own medicine. After being faithful and loyal for years and still not being loved, made a priority or respected as his wife, I opened her heart and legs to another man... a police officer. The one thing I was never able to do was deal with different men at the same time on an intimate level. So, when I let the police officer in, I fell head over heels for him. Of course, he said and did everything that my husband did not, and my mind and emotions were gone. I knew my experience with this man would not last forever. The moments we shared were all lies.

The police officer remarried his ex-wife right under my nose. I was heartbroken. I heard the news from a person I considered to be a spiritual parent, who pretty much threw an uppercut in my chest with this news. Even though I was broken, I moved on. My husband found out about the relationship with the police officer and it broke him as a man. I had never seen him break down and cry. I knew from that point I would never hurt him or anyone else with that type of betrayal. My husband wanted to kill the police officer but thank God others intervened. I let the police officer out of my heart and soul and tried to reconcile with my husband. But my husband became bitter and mean, and refused to forgive me, despite all his faults. So, our marriage ended.

I packed up my two children and moved away. There I was, with two young kids trying to make it on my own. I struggled many days, but still went to school to obtain my first degree, which was a Bachelor's of Science in Social Sciences/Human Services. I decided that I would still go after my dreams. So, in 2012, I moved to Atlanta to pursue a Master's of Science degree in Clinical Mental Health Counseling. Because my biological father suffered from mental illness, I had a passion to help others recover. Throughout my time being single, I came across a con artist who pretended to be a businessman. He was fairly nice, but was fresh out of prison after 25 years. Then, the police officer showed back up in my life, after he divorced his wife. But after the last encounter, I decided not to get involved with the officer again.

My ex-husband started hanging around the family and spending time with the children and me. So, feelings and emotions started to fester again. However, my ex-husband was now engaged to be married to a woman with children and three baby daddies. After my ex-husband discovered that his fiancée was unfaithful by sleeping with her youngest son's father, he decided to let the relationship go and he came back to re-establish a relationship with me and rebuild the bond with his two sons. I asked God to restore our marriage and our oldest son was also asking God the same. God heard the cry and heart of this little boy and put love back between his parents.

Life seemed to be going well, but devasting news was right

around the corner. I discovered that my husband's ex fiancée was pregnant but he assured me that the child wasn't his. Our relationship continued to rekindle and we remarried on Valentine's Day in 2014. A few days after the wedding, my husband told me his ex's baby was indeed his child and it was a girl, making him the woman's fourth baby daddy. Life completely stopped for me. I had just given her heart back to the man who broke it the first time. The one thing I always wanted from my husband was a daughter and he gave his first daughter seed to the street.

The relationship was never the same. However, I stayed with him and had another son in December of 2014. I reached out several times to the mother of my husband's daughter to bring her around her brothers, but the woman refused and that left a little girl without a father. Well, at least that's what I thought. After a conversation with the other mother, I learned that my husband was indeed in his daughter's life and had visited her on several occasions and was still having sex with his ex-fiancée. Okay, I know what you are thinking. Women will say anything just to break up a happy home or get even. But the truth will always be revealed. After my husband refused to get counseling or help for our marriage, I left him for the last time. I decided to re-enroll in school to obtain a doctorate in marriage and family therapy. I also received my counseling license from the state of Georgia.

Still waiting for real love, I decided to love myself and put all the energy that I always put into others, back into myself. I invested myself in my children, my career, and in the world of modeling, acting, and music. This was where my creativity came alive. I finally realized I was born to uplift and inspire others through the arts and through the many talents God gave me.

As I was focusing on my career, what I thought was a man of God named showed up and got my attention. He was packaged perfectly, however my gut told me something wasn't right. I ignored those feelings. I wanted it to be real so I walked away from reality. With lies, deceit and fakeness, he literally took time from my life that I cannot get back. He was seeing another woman while claiming to be grieving the death of a co-worker. While I was praying and crying out to God on his behalf, he was happily dating someone else and that woman posted it on Facebook. I had major choices to make and I decided to move on. After being depressed for weeks, not eating for days, and losing weight, I found the courage to pick myself back up and ran after auditions and other opportunities to occupy my time.

I landed a role in a stage play where I met some interesting people. I wasn't dating and I wasn't entertaining the thought of dating. I was content with it just being my children and me. During one of the rehearsals, a friendly guy named Harrison came in. I ignored him because he was a hippy-looking guy and very free-spirited, which was not my type. I noticed him noticing me, but I ignored the looks. I was sitting center stage and it was his scene. He literally serenaded me with a love song, with direct eye contact. I could not move, blink, or talk. I was mesmerized by what took place. His voice was indescribable. It was a crazy feeling. When I was able to move, I smiled and went on with my night.

Later, he asked for my number and to take our children on play dates together. But the conversation was interrupted and I went home. Harrison was in my inbox asking to spend time with me and complimenting me on my sexiness. He was turning 30 in a few days and asked if he could spend his birthday with me. I agreed and we became friends. After spending a little time together, I searched Facebook and discovered that he was engaged and living with his fiancée, who was helping him raise his son.

I know. I should have walked away. However, I was taken by his voice, his style, and he played the saxophone. He asked me to be his and his fiancée's girlfriend because she liked women. I considered the proposition, but eventually declined because I did not want to accept the role as second, or share. He still pursued me, making all kinds of promises to help me with my music career that had yet to be fulfilled. I eventually walked away when I continued to be disappointed because he did not show up for special moments in my life. Now, I am sure a lot of you women are like, what the hell were you thinking? Let's just say, I wasn't thinking with my brain at all.

After this "situationship", I was done done. I promised myself that I would not be bitter, but to learn from each situation I encountered. I landed several roles, including lead roles in stage plays, and music videos. I also continued to model. I accepted a leading role in a very profound stage play with a handsome co-star named Nehemiah. He was younger, but very mature and business minded. We only wanted friendship from each other, which was very innocent. We talked about life situations and shared a lot of experiences. We spent time together learning our roles and learning each other. I was very reserved and guarded, and he was guarded and respectful towards me. His heart was genuine, and he was honest with me and told me that he was married. He and his wife had made the decision to let the marriage go. As a counselor, I wanted to help Nehemiah through the process, and told him to fight for the marriage if he wanted it to work. He informed me that the decision was made, and the marriage was dissolving. But Nehemiah's wife came after me because she felt that I was the cause of their breakup. Being that I had experienced being in her shoes, the last thing I wanted was to hurt another woman.

After Nehemiah explained everything, I decided to stay by his side through the process, regardless of the bashing of character from his soon to be ex-wife. He accepted the fact that I was a mother, and he did not have any children. However, he wanted me and I wanted him. During one of our evenings together, we shared our first kissed that literally knocked me off of my feet. I struggled to keep my balance after the passionate encounter. The hugs and the intimacy shared between us were unfamiliar for me. I had never known the freedom of joyously enjoying the company of a man, where I could just be myself. His touch is genuinely everything to me, where I intensely craved it. His passion ignites my passion, and when we come together, love explodes. Nehemiah is easy to love because he expresses the love the same way, if not more. I am totally taken by him and will give him what no other woman has - his child. This story is still being written, and the best is yet to come... I hope. Even though this feels so right, I am truly afraid to love again.

I want to end this story by encouraging you to never give up on you. Life happens to all of us and it is not what happens to us that matters, but it's how we handle what happens that matters. Life is a book of experiences that make each one of us uniquely different. Through God, there is absolutely NO-THING we cannot get through or overcome. Your life is worth living and you are worth fighting for.

Tikita Ficklin is a multi-talented gem from Macon, Georgia. The mother of three sons, is an author, singer/songwriter and actress, who has performed in such stage plays as: *From the Pole to the Pulpit; Damnation;* and *The Hem of His Garment.* A licensed professional counselor for the state of Georgia, she relies on her relationship with God to impact the lives of others. Tikita, who earned a master's degree in clinical health counseling, is working on her doctorate in marriage and family therapy. She plans to establish a shelter for homeless families who have experienced domestic violence and other trauma.

MICHELLE S. LOVETT

CHAPTER 6

AMINA KIRK THORNTON
SEATED IN MY ANOINTING

When people hear I grew up in New York, many associate that with the projects, poverty, broken families and other struggles associated with most metropolitan cities. But I'm a product of a strong, influential and well-off family. As a child, I was sheltered, spending most of my time in church, where my grandfather was the pastor. I was supposed to have a stress-free, issue-free, and successful life.

But nobody prepared me to experience the things I endured during this process of becoming who I am today. I've had to deal with pain and betrayal; molestation; rape; the death of my son, Takari, when I was 20 years old; and so much more.

With every situation, I grasped the divine faith that equipped me to overcome all the challenges. I remember the words my grandfather spoke from the pulpit of his church that spanned an entire New York City block. Throughout my life, I have utilized his lessons as well as others in my family as I weighed the good and the bad. Most times, the good outweighed the bad, but much of the bad helped shape my desire to share my story and help as many people as possible.

Everyone knew my family and that brought wanted and unwanted expectations. My grandfather, who everyone called Doctor, was a very tall, distinguished man. I only knew him to be Granddaddy. He was on the Harlem Hospital Board, chaired the New York City Board of Education and was a pillar in the community.

Just the same, everyone knew my daddy. He was born and raised in the community. My mother was Granddaddy's youngest of five. She was an astute educator who aimed high in all her endeavors, graduated with honors, held double master's degrees and spoke multiple languages. All her endeavors were a testament to how much she loved her family and herself. When she did good, we looked good. My father, a career politician, is now retired from the U.S. House of Representatives. Daddy loved and provided for his family as a man should. The worst thing about growing up in the spotlight for me was everyone knew who we were and they were always watching.

My parent's put forth every effort to protect my brother and me, but I became my own worst enemy through the years. Growing up, my family was close. We were always interacting with each other. I had a famous uncle, named John, who was a world-renowned Jazz pianist, composer, arranger and recording artist. After I was grown, I realized I had several famous uncles, some were Silver Star and Bronze Star war heroes. But Uncle John has a New York City Street named in his honor and was named after Granddaddy. Uncle John was often traveling but when he came to town, the house would be full. He always made me feel special. Later, I would come to know that Uncle John always treated my mom special and that was just how he was.

Growing up in a four-story Brownstone, I remember my dad and brother flying kites off the rooftop. I was always told I was too little and that it was too dangerous for me. So, I would find my own danger like the time I managed to get my head stuck between the iron bolsters. It wasn't until I was grown that I saw and appreciated the fortress of love and protection that surrounded me.

Oftentimes, people hold onto pain and use it as a crutch, usually it takes decades or more before realizing our pain is intended to be a tool for our growth and success, it is also intended to draw us closer to God. However, pain often becomes a boulder chained to our future. For a long time, I stood in my own way. Denial is usually the tool that equips us to keep going on the path of our own demise.

I always spent New Year's Eve in church, attending Watch Night service with my family and other faith believers. This one year would be different; I was an inmate in a neighboring county jail. I was assigned to Rooming House One (the other rooming house was for felons and those who posed a threat). Even though we were not considered threats, we all had shackles and cuffs restricting us and leaving cuts and bruises on me. The guards would strip search us and make us squat and cough in an assembly line. They'd toss our space and search them with dogs. All 32 beds were occupied and it became apparent that I would usher in the New Year like never before.

Once reality set in, I recognized that particular New Year's Eve was a pivotal and defining moment for me. Singing songs of Zion while cleaning set a mellow temperament throughout the quarters. And just before the strike of midnight, I was asked to pray. All the women, except for one, assembled in a circle. That moment reminded me of the spirit of a leader that rests upon me and the need for me to kill the flesh for God's plan to move forth.

By then, my husband had finally found me an attorney who was not a crook and had my best interest at hand. My previous lawyer was a former business partner with the judge and I don't know many former business partners who remained in good standing. I didn't know if that would negatively impact me. I was finally done with my pity party, self-starvation and the frequent thoughts of suicide. At one point, my children and the thought of eternal damnation was the only thing keeping me alive. This event was intended to break me, shatter my future and most of all damage my family, but it actually allowed me, as a boulder, to mature into a mountain. There's something attractive about being counted out and still landing on your feet.

Not many knew what was taking place concerning me. I had been very active in my church, including training to be a minister and paying to travel abroad as a Missionary. But I had to leave the training as a result of all the undesirable behavior I was involved in. My husband had been ordained less than two weeks prior to my arrest. Talk about being tested. My husband had confided in some church folks concerning our situation, but he had not spent a lifetime around the church like I had. I was taught there are people you bring home, others you leave in the street and some you still sweep behind after they leave. Despite multiple requests to leadership, serving on several ministries and faithfully paying tithes and offerings, it could not buy me favor with man. Ninety days had passed in the local jail and I never received a visit from one of my local church leaders. I needed a word and I wanted some reassurance that despite my atrocities I still had the favor of God resting upon me. I believe it's important to have the ability to meet people where they are in life and help them along, which piqued my interest to become a certified life coach.

While confined, I woke daily to the birds singing. Eventually, I would rise before the birds and sing soft melodies. My body ached. I lost over 60 pounds, but I didn't look like anything I had been through. The ladies looked up to me and often sought my advice, conversation or prayer and some still refer to me as Godmother. Many of the guards were kind but others had allowed that environment to become who they were.

That place had begun to wear on my body. Thankfully, my mind was sedated and my husband was always available to take my calls and visit me twice weekly over the video phone. In the early stages, I was barely holding myself together, but no one could see through my pride. I had to realize it's never been me holding myself together and my brokenness was a required sacrifice.

Elder Smith, our pastor while we resided in Italy, came to sit, pray and minister to me all the way from Virginia. Our husbands had a tight bond while stationed together in Bahrain and Naples, Italy, where she and I met. Elder Smith left her family without being asked. She will never know how much I needed her and how much the message she delivered meant at that time. After meeting with her, I felt like she was God's reassurance. Not only would God send someone, but it was someone I knew I could trust and it was clear that Virginia was not too far for this King's kid.

Elder Smith, the appointed angel deemed for the assignment, returned once more, months later, shortly following my release. We chilled and had girl time. We stayed in a hotel to easily maneuver to a revival that rendered a spiritual awakening. The following day, we traveled to Alabama for a monumental experience visiting the Legacy Museum and the National Memorial for Peace and Justice. This meant so much to me. It was real ministry. I'll never forget feeling so free that I took my wig off and put it in the back seat as she was driving back to Atlanta.

My great uncle, who was a Silver Star war hero, died the day before my release. Nobody told me because they didn't want me to worry. I wanted to pay my respects, but I also needed a change of scenery and some time to myself. So, less than five days after my release, I traveled to Boston, where a large part of my family resides, and my uncle was laid to rest.

From then on, I continued traveling. I had vowed during confinement that I would not allow grass to grow under my feet. That year, I went to Tennessee with my husband; Boston three times; South Carolina three times; North Carolina twice; Virginia; Washington, D.C., where we spent a week and enjoyed Independence Day; New York City for another week; and I rode the train and bus from South Street Seaport to Queens and traveled all five Boroughs. I traveled to Haiti and the Dominican Republic in the capacity of a missionary. After all, I had vowed to serve for eternity during my time of confinement. I have embarked upon Global Missionary work for over 20 years, traveling and living in Italy, London, Spain, Honduras and most recently traveling to Haiti, Dominican Republic, and South Africa. Each trip proves to be a rewarding adventure. I'm always blessed by God's people and their perspective countries.

My travels abroad begin at an early age and I never stopped going. All my children were born in different countries. This brown girl from New York City will forever be in awe of God. I smashed grapes with my feet to make wine in Sicilian vineyards and swam in the Mediterranean Sea with my cousin, snorkeled in Capri, traveled to The Rock of Gibraltar, and spent a day visiting Morocco by yacht from Costa Del Sol, Spain. I have climbed the Great Wall of China and visited the Terracotta Warriors. I have been to the Caribbean Islands, resided in Puget Sound in Washington State, the most beautiful state of them all. But none of this scratched the surface of the things God has afforded me thus far or all that is to come.

I've been blessed to have traveled the world and each state of the United States has given me a broad perspective about people, their struggles and appreciating the finer things of life. Living abroad for nearly 14 years since the age of 21 is an opportunity that most will never come close to experiencing in their lifetime. Because of my sheltered background, some would think I was wet behind the ears. But being reared in New York City has significant life skills and benefits that have molded and shaped me to methodically maneuver through virtually any situation.

The enemy attempted to take my mind, dissolve my marriage, destroy my family, claim my life, end my profession, declassify me and taint my image. Through it all, I was happy to let go of some unwanted baggage. I also realized other aspects of my life required a facelift so I had to weather the storm.

Life has taught me that no one is immune to tragedy and disaster, regardless of classification. While no one could expect to endure the situations I found myself in, I didn't allow people, things and circumstances to define me. I'm not defined by the tragedies and mistakes that even landed me in jail. I'm not defined by red bottom shoes, Luis Vuitton or Gucci. They are only accessories. I was raised to know who I am and whose I am. Instead of allowing those things to label me, I chose to use them to help me define myself. I am God's child. And I am no longer locked up.

 **Amina Kirk Thornton** was born and raised in New York City. The many crowns she wears are a testament to her ambition and tenacity to be unstoppable. She is educated and trained in the field of dentistry, where she's devoted over a decade of her life serving America's veterans. She has worked for the Atlanta Veteran's Medical Center and Naval Hospitals in California and abroad as a civil service employee. Amina's accomplishments as a United States veteran, military spouse, missionary, entrepreneur, author, CEO of Faithfully Driven, fashionista and certified life coach only scratch the surface of this world traveler's accomplishments.

MICHELLE S. LOVETT

CHAPTER 7

SHAN WHITE
SINGLE PARENT BUT NEVER ALONE

Life as a single parent was so challenging to me. I wish someone had shared a book or something to let me know that the road I was about to go down was not going to smooth. In fact, I was going to need a lot of prayer, if I was going to make it in this life. I had days where I wanted to break down and cry. Sometimes, I wasn't sure if I was even cut out to be a mother. There were plenty of days I just wanted a break, but through it all, I made it. I did what I had to do for my kids. If I had to do it all over again, I would. More than anything, I just wanted the best for them. I wanted to give them a life that I didn't have.

Although my journey was challenging at times, I understand now that it was to help others avoid certain pitfalls and know that they are not alone on their journey. I hope that my story can be a blessing to others and that people who see themselves in my shoes.

As a teenager, I used to love keeping people's kids, especially the little girls because I would braid their hair and put beads in it. I always made sure they were so pretty. I used to say that when I got older, I would have a set of twins and be done with having kids. I thought I was only going to have two. Yet, some things don't turn out how we plan them.

When I was 20, I met a guy name Shawn. He was my brother's friend and co-worker. He always stopped by our house and we argued all the time. As fate would have it, we ended up in a relationship. I saw Shawn every day. When I woke up, Shawn's face would be the first face I saw, and the last face I saw before closing my eyes at night. He'd kiss me on my forehead and go home. Shawn lived with his mother and sister, whom I had known for a while. Sometimes, we would go to his house but most of the time he'd be at my house. We were like two peas in a pod. That's how much we enjoyed being together.

As time went by, my mother noticed a change in me. She kept telling me that I was pregnant. She took me to the doctor, I got a pregnancy test, and it came back negative. I was smiling from ear to ear. My mother said, "I don't know what you're smiling for because you are pregnant." She told the doctor that the test wasn't right because I slept too much. She made him take it again. This time, he performed a blood test instead of a urine test. This time, it came back positive. Not only was I pregnant, the doctor informed me that I had a sexually transmitted disease (STD). I was so confused because Shawn was the only man that I was sleeping with. Somebody had some explaining to do because I needed some answers.

I told Shawn about the baby and I was super excited. I also told him about this STD. He told me that we needed to sit down and discuss it the next day. My phone rings the next day and it's a lady asking me about Shawn and if I was pregnant by him. I was confused. But I learned that the lady and her kids lived with Shawn. It destroyed me. I guess that explained where the STD came from. Minutes later, Shawn walks in the door. This lady was arguing back and forth with him. He eventually told me the truth and the lady packed her items, got her kids and left.

Although I was hurt and very emotional, I was young, pregnant, and in love. I did not want to be without my child's father. So, I stayed with him during my pregnancy and our daughter was born. During my eight-week check-up at the doctor's office, I found out I was pregnant again, this time with a boy.

Shawn stayed in and out of jail... more in jail than out. We had our ups and downs like any relationship, but we managed to get through. He was so loving and could be sweet at times. Even though he did what he did, I forgave him. At some point, we'd separate then get back together like nothing ever happened. But one of the times Shawn was in jail, I got pregnant by another man and had another baby boy, eight years after the birth of my other son. His father was an absent dad but later came around.

Shawn and I eventually talked, and he told me he wanted his family back and wanted to come back home. The following month, we decided to make that happen. He was excited and told everybody he was going home. A week later, I received another phone call from the lady who had been living with Shawn. She told me that he was involved in a tragic motorcycle accident, and loss his life.

God had another plan for Shawn's life and mine as well. I never imagined when he said he was going home that he was going his eternal home, instead of coming home with me and the kids. My live change tremendously that day.

Here I am with three kids who are all depending on me, a high school dropout without a GED. I was concerned that no one would hire me for a decent paying job. At the time I had small jobs that allowed me to keep a roof over our heads and keep some food on the table, but I wasn't making significant money. I was worried.

One day, my kids came home from school asking me to help them with their homework. Because I didn't know the answers, I got so frustrated and took it out on them. I told them they need to stop playing in school. "Go tell your teacher you don't understand," I yelled. "That's her job to teach you. That's what she gets paid for."

Not having an education was just not the move for me any longer. I decided that I was going to go back to school. I went to their school a lot to check on them but more so to learn for myself. I would sit in their classroom trying to learn as much as I could. The teacher would give me a textbook and I would follow along with them. I was going up to the school all the time. My kids hated me being so much. My son used to tell me to go home. He reminded me that I recorded my favorite TV shows so I could go home and watch them. I connected with a couple of teachers and told them what I was trying to do. They were so supportive and helped me study. Lord knows I am so thankful for them. I truly appreciated them more than they will ever now. I ended up taking my high school test. I passed all the classes and graduated with honors. When I held that Diploma in my hand, I cried tears of joy because it was nobody but God. I am a witness of what he can do.

I hear a lot of single moms say they need a man in their life to help raise their kids. I don't believe that's true because God helped me raise my kids. God was my everything and I had to learn to trust and depend on him. After getting that my diploma, I got a job with benefits in law enforcement and I'm still there today. When I got hired, I worked long hours and still do sometimes. I made sure my kids had what they needed.

My daughter enjoyed cheerleading so much that she cheered from age 6 all the way through college. My son played football since he was 6 all the way up from junior high school, in addition to being on the wrestling and swim team. In high school, my son and daughter ran for Mr. & Miss 9th, 10th, 11th, & 12th grade and won. My son won Homecoming King in 12th grade. My daughter had a friend whose mother was going through a tough time so I got temporary custody of the friend and she moved in with us for four years. We treated her like she was family. None of the children wanted for anything.

But sometimes as a single mother, I had to make some difficult decisions and sacrifices. For example, my son was angry with me for years because I missed some of his games. I tried to explain to him that I had to work to be able to afford to give him and his siblings opportunities to play sports. It becomes burdensome sometimes having to buy uniforms and equipment year after year. It adds up. But I made it work because I wanted the best for my children and I wanted them to have those experiences, even if it meant I had to miss some. Those are the types of sacrifices parents should make to keep their children out the streets and in other trouble.

Whenever we needed something, God provided. If we need help from people, God would send them. If we needed resources, he would send them. If we needed money, somehow it all worked out. I was able to send two of my kids to college. My daughter currently works for a popular radio station in Atlanta. My oldest son just graduated from the Navy. My younger son is into computers and will soon graduate high school. I thank God for being there for me and my children.

One thing I want my readers to know. Is that you can do anything you put your mind to it. Be determined to be better.

Believe in yourself and know that God will make a way. As I always tell my kids. To dream big and know that dreams do come true. Sometimes we just got to get out of our flesh and trust God. If God was able to do it for me. Just imagine what he can do for you.

Shan White is CEO and founder of Let's Talk Real Talk and Beauty Beyond Measure. The Atlanta native is an advocate for women empowerment and seeing women succeed in all facets of life. Shan serves as a federal officer with the Department of Homeland Security. Along with being an aspiring actress, who can be seen in plays and short films, Shan loves learning new things and educating herself about things such as with hair and make-up. In addition to starting her own clothing line called GDFAM (God Didn't Forget About Me), Shan enjoys cooking and feeding the homeless.

MICHELLE S. LOVETT

CHAPTER 8

STEPHANIE TAYLOR
PRAY OVER EVERYTHING

My late husband, SSG Jeffrey Carlos Taylor Sr., was the love of my life, my best friend, and my king, who will forever be in my heart. We were married July 17, 1996, one of the happiest days of my life.

We were a young, happy and carefree couple trying to figure out life together. Our focus quickly shifted from us to our children and giving them the lives that would prove to be different from the ones we were raised in. My husband was very strict on education and wanted to make sure that the last choice for any of our children was the military. Today, all our children are doing very well in their school and or college careers. We were a balanced family and encouraged focus as well as creativity in our children. Our home became the home away from home for many people because of the love that was felt throughout.

After many years of traveling and serving in the military, my husband became injured after serving two tours in Iraq. Things in our lives took a drastic change after Jeff returned home the second time and was diagnosed with Post Traumatic Stress Disorder (PTSD). PTSD is often missed, and the trauma is frequently dismissed.

According to Healthy Place for Your Mental Health, anyone can have PTSD, not just military veterans. But veterans have a higher rate of PTSD than that of the general population.

Here are a few interesting PTSD facts is that the statistics on PTSD in the military vary by service era.

- In Operations Iraqi Freedom and Enduring Freedom, between 11-20% of veterans have PTSD in a given year.

- In the Gulf War (Desert Storm), about 12% of veterans have PTSD in a given year.
- About 30% of Vietnam veterans have had PTSD in their lifetimes.

Jeff had to be put on medication. Not long after, I noticed a change in his behavior. He was sleeping constantly, experiencing mood swings and battling depression. I couldn't tell right away what was going on within hi, but it became painfully clear that he was using different outlets to cope with life. After witnessing my husband go through so much anguish, pain and depression, I was faced with the trauma of seeing him overdose for the first time. Unfortunately, that wouldn't be the last time.

I started blaming myself for his behavior, thinking what more could I do to alleviate this pressure I saw controlling him. I would have sleepless nights lying awake to make sure my husband was still breathing. I was doing everything in my power to make sure he kept thriving, but I also was a mother and had responsibilities to my children including school, sports and afterschool activities. One of us had to be there and I was the one. When Jeff showed up, he was overly medicated and couldn't really participate or truly interact with the kids. It was very painful for him, the kids and me. There was a lot of pressure on me. I had to figure out how to continue functioning for both of our roles as parents. My life was falling apart - mind, body and soul.

We were heavily into the church and I began to slip away which is when all hell really broke loose in my life. I had no accountability. I began to get high with my husband and it literally became a living nightmare. Everything I worked for and prayed for to see him through his battle quickly became my battle. I gained so much weight. I got up to 300 pounds, suffered with extreme anxiety and developed fibroids which resulted in me needing emergency surgery, which lead to more medication and more addiction.

There was a time when Jeff and I were both crying out for help. We went to the church but there was such a strong religious spirit that no one was willing to help. But there were many who judged. I believe they thought we had it all together, but little did they know the spirit of death was trying to choke us out. We were barely surviving. One day on, one day off. We both needed to be free from this demon of drugs. But how do we get free?

The first time Jeff overdosed, it scared me so badly that I stopped cold turkey. I watched him in the hospital lying there on life support. I heard the voice of God speak to me in that moment, telling me that I had to pray him through. I wasn't sure how to pray at that time. I was a backslider, literally trying to get out of my own darkness. I was so full of doubt and uncertainty. I remember God using Apostle Cynthia Jefferson to affirm what God had spoken to me in how He wanted me to pray my husband through. She prayed the prayer of Elijah over me. Elijah was a great biblical leader whose power was his ability to stand alone through some seemingly devastating times relying on the power of prayer. (Read 1 Kings for the full story of Elijah. It will inspire you). During this time of standing in the gap for my husband, I felt my faith being restored and strengthened. It felt as if God was restoring and the word of God is true in Deuteronomy 31:6b, He will never leave you nor forsake you.

I began to feel strong enough to pray the prayer of

repentance, forgiveness from adultery, drug abuse and forgiveness for just plain doubting God. I needed clean hands to be able to stand in the gap for my husband. At first, I felt like I couldn't get a prayer through, but God showed up and showed out on our behalf. Every instruction God gave me, I followed it to the point of keeping on my husband's shoes every time I went into his room. This showed me how God could use a mess like me and how powerful having faith in God truly is.

Thinking back, I remember counting the days, naming the days, speaking life into the days as the love of my life, my king, my best friend, lay in that bed. I used to write in a journal every day and day three sticks out I'm my memory. As I wrote Steph and Jeff walking with God, I heard God say, Day 7 Jeff would be off life support, and I believed it. By the power of God, he came out of that coma.

This experience instilled in me the power of prayer to this day. Allow me to share some reasons why I pray, why I will always pray and why I encourage you to increase your prayer life.

- It reveals how we could be the answer to our own requests. When you pray for someone to have comfort during a difficult time, sometimes God whispers that it's your job to be the shoulder they cry on. You have to the be the strength for those around you.
- Praying blesses us in the process of our attempt to be a blessing. When you speak to God on behalf of someone, it can warm your heart knowing what you're doing is important to the kingdom of God. Jeff's soul was important to the Kingdom and because he couldn't speak for himself, I had to.

- It works. Prayers have power. Prayers can work in people's lives in ways you will never be able to fully comprehend. A lot of times, we don't pray big enough prayers. Don't let your small prayers limit what a big God can do. Trust and believe in God's authority.

- Prayer strengthens our communication with God. He wants to hear from his children, and he cares about what is on our hearts. If we talk to God more, then we will naturally be able to hear his answers more than if we had been neglecting Him. Friends don't talk to friends that don't respond. God is the same way. He won't give us revelations every day if we just go through life expecting to hear from him. We must invest in him, too.

- It might show us that we need to be praying the same prayer for ourselves. Often, I pray for healing in someone's life or help for their struggle with a specific sin, only to realize that I need help in the very area as well. God can use our prayers for other believers to reveal their weaknesses that they may be turning a blind eye to.

- Prayer gives us a greater love for the person you pray for. We may not be very fond of someone, but by lifting them up to God, it can change the way we view them. When we talk about someone to God, and ask for their needs to be met, we are looking at them the way God would. We see them out of love and not any negative emotion we may have tied to the thought of them previously. Even if we respect the person, we can gain an even deeper level of care when we ask the God of the universe to work in their life.

Prayer shows us how to give up our own self-knowledge

and methods to receive God's plans for our lives. The more time we spend with someone, the more like them we become. The same goes for our relationship with God. The more fellowship we spend with him, the more we will hunger for him and the things he desires. This will produce a deeper longing for God and time spent in prayer. It's a beautiful cycle drawing our heart ever closer to his.

Jeff and I didn't have a relationship that was perfect. We had our good times and our difficult times. At the end of the day, I have learned a lot from the time we had together. My only regret is that it came to an end too soon. Five years after the first overdose, Jeff overdosed again. This time, he didn't survive. So, I encourage you to always make the most of the moments that you are graced to have with your loved ones and make sure they are okay.

 **Stephanie Taylor** is founder and CEO of Hot Light Entertainment, where she helps others walk in their purpose and showcase their God-given talent. The Detroit native, who was raised in Montgomery, Alabama, but traveled the world as part of her military family. Stephanie graduated from Lanier High School and served as a domestic engineer while traveling abroad with the military. A multi-talented woman, Stephanie is pursuing an acting career and also manages independent artists. In her spare time, Stephanie also enjoys volunteering in schools and churches. She and her late husband, Jeff, had five children together.

MICHELLE S. LOVETT

CHAPTER 9

SCAN JOHNSON
THE JOURNEY TO PEACE

A bad ankle injury my freshman year in college ended my basketball career. My scholarship was rescinded and that essentially ended my college career as well. After college, all my energy went into taking care of my siblings and my second love... music. Since I could no longer play competitive basketball, music became my new first love. My older brother introduced me to a man that owned a recording studio called MindBlowing Records and that's when my music career took off. That's also when I received the name "Scandalous" aka Thug Girl, which I have tattooed on my stomach. I was a force to be reckoned with on the stage and in the streets. I write music about my life, as well as what I go through, so a lot of people can relate to me. I stayed with MindBlowing Records for a few years. I completed two mixtapes with them and did tons of shows. I developed a love for the stage. I wanted to perform more than I wanted to record music. Hitting that stage gave me a rush. I poured all my energy into the crowd. Receiving that energy back made me feel amazing. I used to have a table full of beer that I gave away because I didn't drink at that time.

One day, I was performing in the middle of a crowd because the place didn't have a stage. The energy was so high that four or five guys (white and black) lifted me in the air as I was rapping. That turned me up even more. I was in my element. It was a very memorable day. A few years later, all the fun with MindBlowing ended. The owner was going through a divorce and a lot of stress. He decided to retire for health reasons. I was upset, but it didn't matter because I was focused.

In my mind, I went back to when I was 9 years old and doctors pronounced me dead. I was asleep in the back seat of a car with my older brother. My dad was driving, and my mom was pregnant with her third child. We were riding down one of the busiest streets in the city. My spirit woke me up. All I saw was a car coming full speed out a side street. Everything was in slow motion as the car was coming towards my side of the car. Then BOOM! The car ran right into us, sending us spinning in circles. Everything got quiet for a few seconds then all I heard was people screaming and making strange noises. I remember looking in the rearview mirror at the entire left side of my face split open. It looked like something out of a horror movie. Blood was squirting everywhere. I could see my tongue, my face muscles, and teeth from the side that was split open. There was blood everywhere, but the crazy part is I didn't feel a thing.

The next thing I heard was people trying to get the car doors open, and other bystanders yelling, "Is she dead, is she dead?" My mom responded, "No, my baby ain't dead." Everything went black. I remember waking up in an ambulance with my face and head wrapped in bandages. The only things that weren't covered in bandages were my nose and mouth. I looked over and saw my dad in a bed next to me also wrapped in bandages. My mom and brother trying to get in the ambulance, but it wasn't enough room for them to ride with us. I blacked out again, but this time when I woke up, I was in the emergency room surrounded by family. They were staring at me, some were asking questions, and others were crying. I blacked out again, this time I saw the brightest light that I'd ever seen. All I can say about it was I was at peace. (Later, my mom told me that I was pronounced dead, the pastor prayed over me and I had a heart beat again.)

I found out that the entire back window shattered in my face, which caused all my injuries. They removed all the glass from my face and repaired as many nerves as possible. I was out of school for months and couldn't wait to go back. When I did go back, that's when my life and personality changed. All the teachers were nice to me, but all the kids were mean. They teased me, called me all kinds of names like "ugly" and "scarface". All my excitement that I had for returning to school left.

I cried almost every day, until one day after coming home, my mom was fed up with me crying. She told me she would whoop my ass if I came into the house crying again. I was so upset, but I didn't want her to whoop me so I had no choice but to go to school and defend myself. I had to learn to attack every situation head on if I was going to survive and that became my mentality for life. That's when I learned laser-sharp focus.

My music was the same thing. All I knew was to keep going. I decided to do my own thing. I created my own posters, CDs, and videos. I did anything to get myself shown and known. One day, I was out promoting when I ran into a man who was also promoting himself. He said he appreciated my hustle. He gave me his card, which said he was the owner of Dryksyde Records. I didn't call him until a couple of months later. I was looking for a studio to record so I started looking through my business cards and his popped up. I gave him a call and not long after we got started on my first album, "No Holding Back". He printed and distributed more than 10,000 copies. I was excited because that was a new level for me. I had a real packaged album and we sold most of them. Now, it was time to work on videos. He didn't have the time to do that, but he said his cousin, Shaun, could do it. I had briefly met his cousin before so I was cool with it. The studio was in the basement at his house, so Shaun and I met there to go over the video footage that I had. The man came downstairs and dimmed the lights saying this will help you guys see the footage a little better. I thought it was odd but ok.

Shaun was very cool, proper talking and fresh out of the military. He was very tall and muscular. After his cousin dimmed the lights, we went over everything we needed to but didn't finish so he invited me out to his condo in Wisconsin, which was an hour and a half from where I stayed. He also asked if he could take me to brunch. In my head, I was like, "Brunch!?!" My ghetto butt never heard that word before, but I was smart enough to figure it was lunch mixed with breakfast. I went to his home, we had brunch and that night we finished my promo video. I didn't go home right away because we were having a great conversation. He was such a gentleman. We started talking more on the phone. It became a daily thing. At the time, I was dating someone whom I loved and Shaun was dating a few girls but none was serious. Shaun and I were very different. I was this sexy, drug dealing, hood ass gang leader that was going through a few wars in the hood. Shaun was this tall, handsome black man, with his own place. Later, I learned that he was an electronic engineer. We were both intelligent and into music so the conversations worked. I never talked about the things that I was doing in the streets because none of that mattered when we talked.

Shaun's cousin said he was selling his studio and asked if I wanted to buy it for $6,000. I didn't have that type of money, but I asked him not to sell it and to give me a couple of months to come up with it. At that time, I was working in the barbershop cutting hair. I was working my butt off to get that money. I didn't have all of it but I had most of it. My dad helped me, too. The deadline was approaching for when he wanted to have it sold so I decided to call his cousin Shaun to see if he wanted to put in on this studio and he said yes. From there, we got the equipment, set it up in my mom's basement and I was excited again. Shaun and I went into business together with our label called, Chi City Inc/Common Chord International. We also cleared our closet of the people we were dating and started a commitment with each other. He gave me the code to his home and said any time I need a break or to get away, I could come to his place. I started staying at his place every weekend. It was a break from the streets for me. I used to go there, clean and cook sometimes. He would take me out every time I was there, something I wasn't used to. He kept me smiling. Before he would go to work, he would wake me up and give me a kiss. I was in love with that.

One day, we were at his house lying in the bed. When I woke up, he was staring at me. When I asked him what was wrong, he said, "One day, you're going to wake up married." I told him it wasn't in the plan for me to marry. He simply replied, "Watch."

Our relationship continued and he eventually asked me to move in with him. I told him he lived too far. I was in barber school at the time, trying to run the studio with our artists, hustle, do music and gang bang. I was the princess of the organization. He didn't know about that part. He only knew that I needed to run the studio and had to go to school. So, one day he said he was moving and wanted me to help him find a place on the north side in my city and I agreed. We found him a place and again he asked me again to move in. I said no again but I still stayed with him most weekends. He didn't stay at that place for too long, maybe about six months. I helped him find another place closer to me. This time, I agreed to move in with him. He was very persistent. I knew the place wasn't up to his standards, but he got it so we could be together.

He continued to wake me up with a kiss every morning

before he went to work. I was so in love with him. Eventually, he got tired of that place, too, because it was too far of a drive to his job, so we found a condo that was more his standards and close to the lake. It was very peaceful. In this place, things started off very well. I could tell he was happy. He used to leave $50 on the counter and tell me it was for lunch when I got hungry. It had been three and a half years without feuding. Then, out of nowhere, BAM! It started. I really think the main problem was the commute back and forth. It stressed him out. I couldn't take all the arguing and the name calling so I decided to leave. He ran out behind me, asking me several times to come back. I came back in and that's when he proposed to me. I was very upset, but I still said yes.

Then, he proposed to me with a ring at the studio. I said yes again and we agreed to move somewhere in the middle of his job and where I spent most of my time. He wasn't in Chicago anymore. It was a peaceful environment filled with a lot of things we could do.

We were about six years into our relationship and one year married at this time Everything was all good then once again, it was back to the arguments, fighting and name calling. At this point, we both were unhappy, frustrated and bored. I was too far from Chicago. My mom needed my car to get work so I couldn't just move around when I needed to and that drove me crazy. We weren't cuddling or sleeping in the same room. He became so mean that I thought he was heartless and the devil himself. I used to put holy oil in everything his hands and feet touched. You can laugh but it worked for about a week and every time it would start back up, I would do it again. We were both saying we wanted a divorce. But no matter the situation, he always came in that morning and gave me that morning kiss, even if neither one of us wanted that.

I had dreams. I had goals and I was feeling held back where I was. I wanted to be in Atlanta and I wanted a house. He was making about $30 an hour and was angry at the suggestion of quitting his job and moving to Atlanta. But my spirit was ready to go. I told him I was going whether he came with me or not. The arguing continued here and there. The love just felt like it wasn't there anymore but neither one of us would break it off. Then, on one of our good days, he came in smiling and said, "I put in my two-week's notice." I thought he was lying but he wasn't. I was so excited but that quickly wore off.

A few days later, he told me his job offered him a raise to stay. Something was trying to stay in the way of us leaving and I wasn't having it. Besides, Shaun had already gotten a lead on a job in Atlanta and had an interview scheduled. I called my cousin to see if it was ok if we stayed with her while we looked for a place and she said that it was cool. We made it to Georgia and the job ended up pushing things back because of a government shut down or something. We were going out meeting new people. I was doing my music. He was modeling and acting. Of course, his frustrations always got the best of us. It had been months without an interview. We were living out of this one room at my cousin's house. I was frustrated as well.

Finally, everything seemed to happen at once. He had the job interview, got the job and we found a place of our own. Look at God. The leap of faith is real. Everything was all good, for the most part. We had a swimming pool in the back, a weight room, a 3-mile trail and a pool room. We stayed there for a couple of years and decided it was time to look for the house I had been wanting. It was a task and spooky. Either they were too spooky, too old or too small. Then finally we found this community that said they had no more homes in the area but they do have some in their other community. We went over to check it out, got approved and the next thing I knew, I was picking the section we wanted to live, brick colors, floor, countertops paint, carpet, etc. He told me to pick everything. We were getting our first home built from scratch. I was more excited than ever. We'd been together 11 year through all the ups and downs. I couldn't ask for a better partner. Fortunately, since we'd been in our house, we don't argue or disagree. We are the first spirits that's been in this house. Today, we continue to love each other unconditionally, grow with each other and separately (as far as our careers and different companies). We continue to find our peace.

 **Scan Johnson** was born and raised on the south side of Chicago. An internationally recognized recording artist who received the name Scandalous because of her raw rhyme abilities, confidence and commanding stage presence, she exhibits versatile rhyme styles, innovative concepts and real-life intriguing content. She has a way of capturing your heart and soul. Her music and writing mirror her most extreme dealings with the realities she experienced through life. Scan enjoys traveling, playing basketball and exploring new adventures. She and her husband reside in Atlanta.

MICHELLE S. LOVETT

CHAPTER 10

SHELBY FRASIER
SHE'S FINALLY HERE

I was born September 16, 1991, in Atlantic City, New Jersey. At a very young age, I attended Mont Zion Baptist Church with my grandparents. By the time I was seven and heard the music and voices from the choir, I wanted to be a part. At 10, I joined the church choir. Later that year, my grandmother was teaching adult Sunday school and asked my sister Nikki and me if we wanted to sing each time she taught. My sister and I would sing, bringing smiles and joy to the people in the class.

I was brought into a family that loved, cared and nourished our dreams and goals. As the years went on, I experienced so much pain. In 2004, my grandmother passed away from lung cancer; my cousin was shot that same year; 2007 my Uncle Billy had a stroke; and my paternal grandmother passed away. I knew that the family was never going to be the same.

The morning of my high school graduation in 2009, I was sick in the hospital. I was scheduled to sing at graduation and didn't know how I was going to do it. Somehow, God pulled me through it. When asked what I wanted to do with my life after graduation, I said I wanted to be a performer because I loved to sing and act ever since I played Dorothy in The Wiz. I remember my director, Kevin Chatham, asking me, "Shelby, is this what you want to do?" I was nervous but I replied, "Absolutely!"

I never understand why people push others to find a safe path when sometimes your passion and life calling takes you in a different direction. It's my life and if I stumble along the way, I know I have to get back up and keep going. I was upset when people tried to discourage me from pursuing my dreams. I wanted more support. I needed more support. My father was the right person for that job. He always encouraged me. He'd say, "Chase your dreams, Shelby. Don't let nobody stop you. Be your own boss."

One day I came home from hanging with my friends and my father handed me a brochure from the American Musical and Dramatic Academy of New York City (AMDA). He said, "Shelby, why don't you go here." Without hesitation, I said yes and that day we set up an audition. As I prepared for my audition, I was a little scared. New York, the Big Apple, was the city where dreams are made. I didn't know what to expect but I was excited. I did everything I could to prepare and just went for it.

As I entered in the room for my audition, the director told me to slate my name and acknowledge what piece I would be performing. I stepped up with confidence. "My name is Shelby Frasier and I will be doing a monologue from *A Raisin in the Sun* and will be singing Home from The Wiz." I took a deep breath and began. When I started to sing, I was looking at the judges faces. They were stoic. There were no smiles, no emotions, nothing. They thanked me, I thanked them and I walked out the door. My parents were in the waiting area. I told them I felt good about my performance despite not getting any reaction from the judges.

Some time had passed and my father kept asking if I had heard anything from AMDA. When I said no, he told me to call them. I was so anxious and nervous but I called. They informed me that I had been accepted and that I would receive an official acceptance letter in a few days. I thanked them and ran straight to my parents with the great news. "I did it!" I yelled. We were all extremely excited.

My first semester of college was exciting. I met some

amazing people who had the same goals. We were taught the right way to audition, the ins and outs of the business side of entertainment, and all the intricacies of what being a performer was all about. I was already living a dream.

Right after receiving my midterm grades, I got a call from my mother. I was ready to tell her all about that I had done well so far and I heard the crackling in her voice as she began to cry. I didn't know what was happening. She told me my Pop Pop died. My head immediately started hurting. I screamed and dropped the phone. How could this happen. My grandfather was supposed to be with me all the way through this journey. He and my grandmother helped me to get to the school. I was numb. All I could do was call on God to help me.

My counselor picked me up from the ground and took me in the office. I told her I needed two weeks to be with my family. She asked me what I would do if I had a show scheduled and something like this happened. I told her that because of an emergency, I would have to take the time I needed to be with my loved ones. I left the office to pack.

When I came back from my grandfather's funeral, it pushed me to complete school. Even though I failed a class that semester, it didn't stop me. I was determined to overcome all obstacles. And I did. I graduated AMDA. It was one of the proudest moments of my life.

A year or so later, my heart was crushed again, this time by the man I loved. I found out that the man who was my everything, the one that I trusted in and confided everything to, cheated on me and got another woman pregnant. Thinking he was different from the other guys I had dealt with, I put down guard and opened my heart to him, only to have it snatched from me and stomped on. But as big as my heart is, once you hurt it, there is no coming back from it. So, I had to deal with the pain and move on.

I left AMDA in New York and enrolled in the AMDA in Los Angeles to bachelor's degree in fine arts. My father suggested it and I thought it was a great idea. I was going to make the best of it. I loved LA just like I loved New York.

I returned to New Jersey eager to start my career. Being a recent college graduate was hard. I would cry at night because I didn't have money. My father saw how depressed I was and helped me get a job at Red Lobster, but of course I still auditioned. Even though I wasn't booking anything thing, I kept believing and keep submitting. One day, my friend Holly told me about an audition for a tour. I quickly picked my song and was on my way back to my loveable city of New York. As we waited in the waiting room, I heard my name called and I headed straight to the door. I entered and felt right at home. I performed my song and went back to the waiting room. Names were announced for callbacks and mine was among them. I was so excited. I started to pull sheet music out my book since I hadn't rehearsed another song. I entered the room again and they asked to see my book. After flipping through it, one of the casting agents told me to sing Big Black Lady Stops the Show by Martin Short Fame Becomes Me. Unlike my initial audition for AMDA when there wasn't an emotion of the face of anybody, this time I had the panel smiling and laughing. I left the room with a smile on my face as well. I knew this opportunity could really change my life.

The next day was the dance call. I performed and left feeling like I did well. I didn't hear anything back but it didn't discourage me. I just remained focused and pushed harder. Months later, I had just finished two shows of Growing up in the Other Atlantic City, an original play about a famous, family-owned restaurant, and The Color Purple. I wanted to do more.

The opportunity presented itself for me to move to Atlanta with my girls Kiyana and Lee Lee. We didn't hesitate and left that week. Atlanta was a fresh start for all of us, especially me. I knew the transition wasn't going to be easy but I was ready to network and see what this new opportunity had in store for me. My parents didn't think it was a good move for me but I believe that it was the best move for me. At the time, I had been seeing a new guy whom I had been spending a lot of time with. So, when he found out about the move, it hurt both of us.

But this new start was just what I needed. I met new people, I learned the friendly southern way, and I continued to pursue my goals. About a year into being in Atlanta, I started getting sick. I didn't know what was going on. I kept calling off work or I would get sent home if I got sick while I was there. But I was so stubborn that I tried to hide it from people, including my managers who suggested I go to the hospital. All I wanted to do was sleep and be left alone.

One day, I passed out at work. It scared me. I thought I was never going to wake up. I had to know what was going on with me. I found out I was anemic. I had been eating a lot of ice and was always tired. Some things were starting to make a little sense. But because of all the time I was missing from work, I got behind on my bills and I was struggling. I tried to find another job. After going on interview after interview, I couldn't take it anymore. I cried to my father, admitting that maybe he was right about Atlanta not being a good move. But I knew I had to keep pushing.

One day, I received a call saying that my aunt was in the hospital not far from where I was in Atlanta. I called an Uber and went to see her. She had a stroke but thankfully she was going to be ok. But it was still difficult telling my father about what my aunt experienced. But like always, he had a way of making me smile.

I'll never forget the call I received from my father on November 18. He told me he went to a theater in Philly and gave them my information. I asked why he would do that knowing I was in Atlanta. I knew he didn't mean any hard. He only wanted what was best for me and wanted me to be successful. But we had a little disagreement about it and he said he would call me back. When the phone rang again, it was his number but a lady was on the phone. She asked if I was the daughter of Larry Frasier. I said yes. Before I could ask who she was, she said, "I'm sorry but your dad passed away." My heart dropped and shattered in a million pieces. I never could have imagined that that would be my last conversation with Daddy. I dropped the phone and collapsed to the floor with it. I couldn't believe what I had just heard. Kiyana comforted me as best she could.

That night, I knew I couldn't stay at my house. Still in shock, I went to my uncle's house and collapsed in my aunt's arms until I cried myself to sleep.

A year went by since I lost Daddy, my supporter and best friend. I moved in with my Uncle Karl. Still grieving my father's death and having financial problems had me very depressed. I wasn't eating and was sleeping a lot. I was barely working. I was grateful for my family's help but I was no longer myself. I felt locked up in my mind. I wanted to die. My aunt and uncle encouraged me every day. My aunt prayed and said doors would open up for me but I had to be prepared to walk through them. Sure enough, God enlightened me and sent an angel. I was introduced to a beautiful soul by my favorite manager, Ms. Heather. She introduced me to people in the entertainment industry because she believed in me. Then, I was introduced to Michelle Lovett. She instantly became my big sister and took me under her wing. I went with her to a play rehearsal and there Ms. Beverly told a chance on me to be a part of the play. I knew that God never left my side. With his help and the people that he placed in my life, I was finding my way back to freedom. I was becoming myself again. I determined that I was going to be the success that I always dreamed about and that my father believed I would be. I never thought I would survive the hurt and pain I did but now I understand that my experiences were designed to help others get through their difficult moments. So, no matter what you go through, remember it is for a reason. It may hurt in the moment, but you will succeed in the next season.

 **Shelby Frasier** was born to be a star. Her passion for the arts started in church. Later, she studied performing arts at the American Musical and Dramatic Academy of New York and Los Angeles. The Atlantic City, New Jersey, native has performed in such productions as The Wiz, Little Shop of Horrors and The Color Purple. Shelby moved

to Atlanta to pursue her dreams of being in the entertainment industry. Among her hobbies are: shopping; traveling; performing community service projects; crocheting; and writing monologues.

EPILOGUE
MICHELLE S. LOVETT

God woke me up one morning saying move and I did. At first, I was a bit startled because some of the decisions. Naturally, I don't question God. However, some reservations surfaced because I didn't know some of the ladies. God had chosen me to breathe life into some, resurrect others, build, motivate and bond with them all. Early on, I realized "curator" was not going to be my only title or duty. I am known for staying on the scene and in the know. My business name and persona is "MEME ALL OVER". The lifestyle I envisioned for some of the ladies was far-fetched. Several began to adapt and now are ready to move and shake. Some ladies, unfortunately, remain locked up, while others are treading water.

Life, Love and Lockup Volume 1 – We Got Work to Do consists of 10 women with different personalities, from different places around the globe and different socio-economic statuses. Our first photoshoot was extra chaotic and I almost gave up. Every facial expression, body language and behavior came across sad, tired, depressed and overall "LOCKED UP"! Our branding consultant Russell Tyson automatically zoned in. He told me that heat and pressure are what make diamonds and convinced me not to worry.

We all had areas where we lacked confidence or struggled with. At that point, I realized I needed them and they needed me. It was then time to bond. We would meet, eat, fellowship and enjoy the camaraderie at the Hilton. We shared our different journeys with one another. The information provided assessments concluding with each individual's status, (Free, Probation, Halfway or Locked Up). As I began to hear the testimonials, my emotions became heavy. Everyone was wearing masks, yet they were walking around like they had it all together. They constantly asked how do I cover my stomach and did you take my picture on my good side? There were plenty other examples but these stood out the most.

I had to make a decision: Be like Isaiah in the bible and tell these young ladies, "Baby, y'all are headed for self-destruction!" or take it all to God in prayer? I went to God and he gave me direction and glimpse of what things would look like by the time the project was completed.

Everyone's chapter relates to me at some point in my life. My smile came at a cost. I've cried for many years, sometimes even in my sleep. I experienced mental, physical and spiritual abuse. That's when I was able to identify when others were masking or hiding behind their pain because she looked just like me. As a woman with several confessions, I was once forced to write a letter when I was able to unplug my obsessions to unlock my freedom. I prayed over everything as I took the journey to my peace.

This journey is not always easy. True success causes separation from many, especially those who wish you well publicly but really wish you hell in private! I can hear someone asking me, "How do I determined who those people are?"

Some people will show their hand of hate, jealousy and envy! You must watch their behavior, use your instinct, vibes or situations. I deal with it all and the best advice I can give us this is: At all times, I remain prayed up, unbothered, booked and busy!

Oftentimes, the people who create chaos in your life don't care about hurting anyone's feelings, emotions or damaging other people's character.

Their main objectives are to tell *their* story and receive buy-ins from listeners who believe what they say is reliable! They team up with others like themselves, turn the story into a script, or sometimes a book that may or may not become a best seller. Meanwhile, the audience continues to grow and the writer continues to write. Before you know it, the script becomes a stageplay and the actors now become unintentional enablers because it seems to be getting good now! A short film is created and posted for the public to see. Viewers are increasing! The audience is growing. Before you know it, the story becomes a number one movie!

But in many cases, the people who are doing the heavy lifting (helping to develop the projects with substance, increasing the audience, and bringing credibility) are treated like workers rather than family. They are not encouraged to branch out on their own, build their own brands, or birth purpose in their own lives. Doing so becomes a threat to some and causes hostility and animosity.

So I understood how the ladies of *Life, Love and Lockup* brought their own issues, flaws and insecurities to the table. We all became vulnerable. We had to learn ourselves and one another. We had to trust ourselves and one another. That's why our bonding meetings and activities were so important to me. We had to learn that it was ok to remove the masks and know that the ladies taking this journey with us were not out to harm them but to build them up and give them the tools and resources for them to no longer be locked up.

Yes, God gave *me* the assignment to go get these ladies and present this opportunity for us all to win. It's not about me. It never has been. It's about all of us. These diamonds had to relive some painful experiences, overcome some trust issues, and battle the demons that wanted to keep them locked up. Their journeys have helped me in so many ways when I thought I was just supposed to help them. So, I am glad I didn't give up on the project when times got tough. I pressed on and so did these ladies. And I'm confident that because they were able to tell their stories, you have been blessed, too. I hope this encourages you to take inventory of your life, begin the process of ridding yourself of the baggage that has prevented you from moving forward, and to take the journey to no longer be locked up.

ABOUT THE COMPILER

Michelle S. Lovett is the visionary behind Life, Love and Lockup. She was born premature, with a heart murmur, severe allergies and battling chronic asthma on September 7, 1976, at Homestead Air force Hospital in Homestead, Florida, to Bennie and the late Gloria Lovett. At one point, doctors declared death at birth. From Day 1, Michelle had to fight.

Nothing has deterred her from pursuing her dreams of becoming an A-list actor, author, entrepreneur or giving back in the process. Since the age of 4, Michelle has been able to remember and recite extended material in church and school productions. People always told her she was extremely talented and gifted, but that gift was put on the back burner for years.

The Miami native, the youngest of six children in a blended family, spent a lot of her youth in church watching her parents serve. She followed their footsteps, serving on the usher board, singing in the choir and participating in holiday productions. It was also through her parents' examples that she excelled in school, was active in the community, inducted into the National Honor Society (college), gifted programs and held several leadership positions.

Upon graduating high school, Michelle enrolled at Paine College. The transition was challenging, eventually leading her to Georgia Military College where she earned an Associate's degree in criminal investigations. Later, she enrolled at Albany State University completing all courses in criminal justice. One of her dreams was to become a judge so she could positively impact the community. Later, she earned a Bachelor's degree in criminal justice from Strayer University.

Michelle spent 10 years working in the financial industry, climbing the ranks and holding leadership roles as a conversion specialist, manager and fraud investigator. Michelle's entrepreneurial mindset soon re-emerged. She watched her parents run several successful businesses. Michelle combines her learning and corporate managerial skills from the bank in 2012 and opened MEME'ENT, an entertainment company, managing independent artists and promoting events. Late 2014, she opened and operated TEAMUP TRUCKS, a trucking company.

Michelle, re-evaluated life and what she wanted from it. She walked away from the corporate world, slowed operations on the trucking company, and found a special joy working in the entertainment industry. In 2015, Sista Girl London offered her a role in her stage play and she returned to acting. But in 2016 and 2017, she struggled and battled with lupus. Doctors gave her six months to live. She was forced to stop acting. Michelle, started a new regiment and began living a holistic lifestyle.

Two years later, GOD proved once again that Michelle is his child. She was alive, healthy and death wasn't in the forecast. She returned to the stage, television, and film, gaining acting experience and quickly becoming a sought after actor in the

Atlanta area. She has done background work for television shows such as Black Lightning, Cobra Kai, BET Tales and Tyler Perry's commercial for his last stage play. Michelle has also starred or co-starred in eight stage plays, including Where's My God Man written by Evans Louissaint; Damnation written by Russell Tyson; How to Love a Damaged Man written by SistaGirl London; and True Love written by Beverly Banks. Admiring such actors as Denzel Washington, Regina King, Gabrielle Union and Tiffany Haddish, Michelle sees herself sharing scenes with them soon.

Today, Michelle is a radio host, author, actress, and CEO of MemeAllOver and Life, Love and Lockup. In her spare time, she enjoys writing; studying acting; traveling; spending time with family and friends; and researching natural products and information; and continuing her fight against lupus. She resides in Atlanta, GA.

MICHELLE S. LOVETT

LIFE, LOVE & LOCKUP

LIFE, LOVE & LOCKUP
www.lifeloveandlockup.com

MICHELLE S. LOVETT

69247204R00070

Made in the USA
Columbia, SC
19 August 2019